God Knows
Life Gets
Hard

God Knows
Life Gets
Hard

10 Tips for Tough Times

Marilyn Kielbasa

SORIN BOOKS   Notre Dame, Indiana

www.avemariapress.com

International Standard Book Number: 1-893732-68-1

Cover and text design by Katherine Robinson Coleman

Printed and bound in the United States of America.

Library of Congress Cataloging-in-Publication Data
Kielbasa, Marilyn.
  God knows life gets hard : 10 tips for tough times / Marilyn Kielbasa.
    p. cm.
  ISBN 1-893732-68-1 (pbk.)
  1. Perseverance (Ethics) 2. Conduct of life. I. Title.
BJ1533.P4K5 2004
248.8′6—dc22

                                        2004009941

Special Thanks

I am deeply grateful to those who shared their stories with me or allowed me to draw on incidents where our lives and spirits intersected. I simply could not have done this book without the contributions of the following people:

Jaclyn Chentfant, Lackawanna, New York

Janet Claussen, Atlanta, Georgia

Annmarie Demarais, Winona, Minnesota

Khristopher Grant, Winona, Minnesota

Rose Hauser, West Seneca, New York

Carl Koch, Onalaska, Wisconsin

Alice Kuder, Seattle, Washington

Jennifer Marshik, Lackawanna, New York

Victoria Marshik, Lackawanna, New York

Esther, Henry, and Lucy Moss, Sioux City, Iowa

Linell Gray Moss, Sioux City, Iowa

Joan Peck, West Seneca, New York

Tom Scherr, West Seneca, New York

Susan Speraw, Knoxville, Tennessee

Sam Wilt, Arlington, Massachusetts

Mark Wilant, Winona, Minnesota

Eileen Wolosz, Bakersfield, California

Tom Zanzig, Madison, Wisconsin

Mary Ellen Zenka, Beaverton, Oregon

Other contributors preferred not to be identified, but I am no less grateful to them. Several other people offered stories that I was not able to use in the book; they too receive my thanks.

Special thanks to my editor, Carl Koch, for his patience, encouragement, affirmation, support, and for a lot of things that he *did not* do or say.

And finally, to—and for—my family, I give profound thanks.

CONTENTS

Introduction

THE HUMAN CONDITION DESCRIBES
THAT DECADES-LONG PREDICAMENT OF
PASSION AND PAIN
IN WHICH WE ALL FIND OURSELVES—
BORN MORE ALIKE THAN DIFFERENT,
PROCEEDING MORE DIFFERENT THAN
ALIKE,
LIVING TOGETHER AND DYING ALONE.

Marilyn vos Savant

As one friend remarked, it was a most forgettable summer. It was my first summer back home after thirty years of being away. I moved back for lots of good reasons, but after almost a year I came to the conclusion that though it was the right thing for me to do, I was not all that crazy about returning to the corner of the world I grew up in. I missed my old life. It was a good life: productive, busy, familiar, and contented. Although I was back in the house I grew up in, my new life was a lot more uncertain, unsettled, and unfamiliar.

Then things got worse. My mom fell down the basement stairs, breaking her leg in two places—a feat that landed her in surgery. After a five-day detour through the

cardiac intensive care unit, a few more days on the
orthopedic floor, and some time in a rehab facility, Mom
came home, only to be wheelchair-bound for three months.
It was going to be a challenge for this woman in her mid-
seventies, who was not used to being sedentary or
dependent.

Mom and I live in an old house—the house she and
Dad moved into when I was six months old. As with most
old homes in the northeast, it has narrow doors, lots of
stairs, one tiny bathroom with a tub (but no shower), and
halls that barely allow passage of a fully-grown human
being, let alone a wheelchair, walker, and other medical
paraphernalia. It was a physical, emotional, and logistical
challenge for all of us—me, Mom, my siblings, and lots of
other family members who pitched in that summer as
caregivers and companions—but we were making it work.

Then things got worse. I had agreed a few months
earlier to teach a ministry course in a city some distance
away. The director and I agreed on three three-and-a-half
hour meetings to cut down on the number of times I would
have to make the almost two-hundred mile round trip. I
carefully checked my schedule before I agreed to teach this
course on three consecutive Tuesday nights. As a
freelancer, I welcomed the work, even though I dreaded
the travel. I looked forward to being with ministry
professionals on a regular basis. Finances had been tight
since I left my full-time job and I relied on the revenue I
received from teaching, consulting, writing, and doing
workshops for people involved in youth ministry. I also
received a small but steady income from my position as a
piano teacher.

A few days before the first class, someone called my
attention to an apparent discrepancy: The course that I

agreed to teach on *Tuesday* had been scheduled and advertised for *Wednesday*. It couldn't be! I had a full docket of piano students on Wednesday! Relatives had arranged their schedules to be with Mom on Tuesdays. I had given my fifteen-year-old niece a birthday gift of four weeks in the zookeeper apprentice program at the local zoo—along with a promise to her working parents to provide the transportation. The program was held Wednesday through Saturday.

But all my careful planning was for naught. Though the director apologetically acknowledged that the mistake was on his end, twenty-one people were expecting to take a course on three consecutive Wednesday nights. My only choices were to bail out or to try to make it work. In my mind, bailing was not an option. After rescheduling piano lessons, making new transportation arrangements for my niece to and from the zoo, and finding people to be home with mom, we were making it work.

Then things got worse. I woke up one morning with excruciating pain in my leg. Maybe it was from all the stress of the past months; maybe it was hauling and hoisting the walker, the wheelchair, and my mom once too often; maybe eight months of long, brisk, nightly walks with our overzealous miniature schnauzer were finally taking their toll. Whatever the reasons, I hurt. I could not sleep; I could not sit; I could not lay. Those daily trips to the zoo and back became tests of pain-bearing endurance. It took an hour longer than usual to get to my last Wednesday night class because I had to stop several times and walk off the pain. When I finally saw a doctor, he simply confirmed my suspicions: I had severely strained the muscles in my upper leg. It would take time to heal. I couldn't do as much for and with Mom as I had before, but with the help of the rest of the family we made it work.

Then things stopped getting worse. My niece completed the zoo apprentice program without missing a day. The final reflection papers from my students revealed that they gleaned a lot more from our time together than I ever suspected I gave them. Piano lessons soon got back on schedule. Mom adapted well to the changing schedule, and our schnauzer was content with walking half the usual distance at half the usual pace.

Many Other dilemmas and minor disasters made me think the summer would never end. I just wanted to get on with my life. Then I began realizing that this *was* my life. However, when I thought about the events of those months, I realized that nothing major had happened. Other than Mom's accident—which was by no means life-threatening—no crisis had occurred. What had happened was a series of mishaps that affected my life in adverse ways and created challenges to my familiar way of being. My friend was correct when he dubbed it "a most forgettable summer," but forgetting it is the last thing I need or want to do.

I want to hold onto the memory of surviving, of making things work, of reaching out for help, of making constant adjustments, of finding inner strength, and of getting through. I want to remember that there were many gifts that would have been ignored had life gone smoothly for those few months, and what it felt like to recognize hopeful signs along the way. I want to hold onto these things because I *know* something like this will happen again. I know it will happen again because it's happened before. It's happened to everyone I know. It's happened to you.

Sometimes the tough times are more than a series of mishaps or challenges in a person's life that, when strung together, make life difficult to handle. Many people live in environments where obstacles are relentless and hurdles are the norm. Real crises bring about profound and radical changes and the emotional struggles that accompany such events. Putting one foot in front of the other requires superhuman courage. Even these times—and maybe these times most of all—provide life lessons and grace-filled moments.

The stories contained within—which are both true and real—are my stories and your stories. Though the details may change, the struggles and the lessons remain the same. *God Knows Life Gets Hard* is a book for every human being on the planet that suffers from and celebrates the wondrous mystery we call "the human condition."

NORMAL IS JUST A SETTING ON YOUR DRYER.

Patsy Clairmont

1

Acknowledge Your Struggles

IT'S A SHALLOW LIFE THAT DOESN'T
GIVE A PERSON A FEW SCARS.

Garrison Keillor

One warm summer morning, four-year-old Henry encountered a large black bug meandering around in the red Radio Flyer he wanted to use for collecting rocks that day. He called to his mother who came out and surveyed the situation. She made a number of suggestions for dealing with the issue; he could turn the wagon over and dump the bug out, find something else to use for collecting rocks, or capture the bug and let it loose in the grass. Henry summarily rejected every suggestion. Finally exasperated, he said in a strong voice "But, Mom, that won't solve the *problem*!" He retrieved some scraps of wood from the garage and proceeded to block off a section of the wagon bed so that the bug could continue its meandering, albeit in a smaller area. Henry then began his morning task, using the rest of the wagon for his rock collection.

Henry had a problem; in his four-year-old wisdom, he knew that if he tried to ignore it by finding something else in which to collect rocks, he would keep coming back to his wagon, which is the tool he really wanted to use that day. If he dumped the bug out or captured it and set it free, he knew that his curiosity would get the better of him and he would go in search of it. Instead, he acknowledged that he had a problem, made accommodations for it within his life, and went about his business.

Acknowledging that we sometimes struggle with life is the first step toward handling adversity. But in a culture where independence and self-reliance are prized, we often deny the fact that we carry burdens from day to day. We ignore the problems, or we make light of the ways they impact our lives. If we let ourselves think about our day-to-day challenges, we may look at other people and the struggles they face and feel guilty for dwelling on our own. We see people in crisis and thank God that we are not like them. But as human beings we experience all kinds of hurdles in life, and these obstacles can be an impediment to happiness.

Most of our struggles fall into one of three categories: *challenges*, *changes*, and *crises*. The difference between each category is in the intensity and abruptness of a situation. First we must admit that a problem exists, then decide what type of struggle we are looking at. Classifying the problem can help us make decisions and take actions that will help us cope, and ultimately help us grow.

Challenges: Most of the everyday struggles we face fall into this category. Challenges are interruptions to a familiar or ideal way of being. Keep in mind what the cartoon *Dilbert* said: "Accept that some days you are the pigeon, and some days the statue." Sometimes challenges are the irksome drone of life, and we feel and even act like the lone statue at the mercy of a flock of pigeons. At other times challenges spur us on to do and to be our best, even though the situation still poses a challenge to our familiar way of being. This category might include a confrontation with someone, a minor illness or accident, dealing with a recalcitrant teen at home, a job-related deadline, impossible family schedules, a difficult relationship, or a financial setback.

Recognizing challenges for what they are means being able to weave them into our life, just as four-year-old Henry accommodated the bug in his Radio Flyer. The results may be positive or negative depending on how we handle them and how they affect our life.

Changes are unavoidable in life, and they are usually unwelcome. Changes can affect us in adverse or in positive ways, but in either case change is stressful and can impact us physically, emotionally, spiritually, intellectually, or socially. Changes can result from natural occurrences, such as a pregnancy, illness, or aging. Or they might be situational changes, such as starting a new job, moving to a new home, taking on the role of caregiver, sending a child off to college, or the onset of a permanent disability. Emotional and spiritual changes also cause upheaval in our lives. Growing apart from an old friend or a spiritual awakening are examples of changes that often catch us off guard, no matter how prepared we think we might be.

Crises are sudden, unexpected, or serious turning points in life. We are least prepared for these events, yet they cause the greatest amount of adversity. Crisis moments include a death, a serious illness or accident, a divorce, termination from a job, a violent encounter, or any situation that results in tremendous emotional or spiritual upheaval.

For most people, it is easy to recognize a real crisis and easy to admit that life seems tough at the moment. Most people experience only a few real crises in their lifetime. The aftermath of crises—the day-to-day problems that result from such events—generally fall into one or both of the other categories: challenges and changes.

A children's riddle asks, "How far can you walk into a forest?" The answer: "Halfway. After that you're walking out." Acknowledging that we are in "the forest" allows us to really think about where we are, so that we can begin the journey out. Knowing the name of "the forest"—challenge, change, or crisis—helps us get our bearings and equip ourselves. Just like Henry with the bug in his wagon, when we arm ourselves with acknowledgment and self-knowledge, we can adapt the Radio Flyer that is our life for the journey ahead.

ANY IDIOT CAN FACE A CRISIS. IT IS THIS DAY-TO-DAY LIVING THAT WEARS YOU OUT.

Anton Chekhov

Acknowledge Your Struggles

- Think about advice for dealing with tough times you have received through the years. Which suggestions helped you cope with your struggles? Which ones were detrimental to you? Have you given advice to others?

- Make a table of any struggles you are in the midst of experiencing or have recently experienced, classifying them under the headings of challenges, changes, and crises. How do these lists compare in length? Does seeing the lists on paper help put things in perspective? Why or why not?

- Write a letter to one of your challenges or changes. Explain how it affects you in adverse ways. Acknowledge that you will live with this situation, but emphasize that you will not let it get the best of you.

- Search for music, art work, or texts that speak to you about overcoming adversity. Keep these things handy and listen to, view, or read them when things are tough.

- In the Christian Scriptures, Jesus says, "Come to me, all you that are weary and are carrying heavy burdens, and I will give you rest. . . . For I am gentle and humble in heart, and you will find rest for your souls" (Matthew 11:28–29 NRSV). What burdens do you want to place before your higher power? Visualize yourself slowly giving over the challenges of your day to open, willing hands. Notice how each is accepted—and you are accepted—gently and lovingly.

THE WORLD BREAKS EVERYONE, AND
AFTERWARD, MANY ARE STRONG AT THE
BROKEN PLACES.

Ernest Hemingway

Changing Horses Midstream

When someone asks what I do for a living, I preface my job description with a joke about being "vocationally schizophrenic." Or I might say something about being a dual-career household in spite of the fact that I'm single and have lived alone for most of my adult life. Then I explain that, until recently, I worked full time in church ministry and related fields, while I also worked as a full time musician and music teacher. Developing and managing parallel careers is second nature to me now, though it is not without its challenges. Learning to switch back and forth between jobs on a daily basis, "changing horses in the middle of the stream," has brought many moments of panic, self-doubt, worry, and struggle.

Growing up, music was what I loved most of all in life. No one was surprised when I decided to major in it in college; nor were they surprised when I decided to head to graduate school to pursue a doctorate in musicology. I had a successful academic career and managed to eke out a living as a teaching assistant at the university I attended, while also working in the music library and taking occasional part time teaching jobs at area colleges.

One Sunday I read an announcement in the church bulletin asking for people to help out with the high school religious education program. I volunteered and was assigned a partner and a group of tenth graders. It was a new challenge for both of us, and my partner teacher and I embraced it wholeheartedly.

For me it was a wonderful diversion from the world of academia, but my priority was finishing my Ph.D. Slowly and steadily I worked my way through the academic hoops of course work, dissertation proposals, piano recitals, and doctoral qualifying exams. With all that behind me, the last link between dream and reality was a dissertation. "Viennese Magic Opera in the Late Eighteenth Century" was my topic of choice. Then it happened: the thrill of a lifetime—a Fulbright grant to spend a year in Austria. I was sorry to say goodbye to my volunteer work at the parish, but I would return when the year was up.

The year I lived in Vienna was wonderful in so many ways, but there was a growing suspicion that I was not living the life I was intended to live. On a snowy February day I received a newsy letter from my partner teacher filling me in on parish happenings and family life. At the end of the letter she reported that the youth minister had decided to leave her job at the parish and jokingly asked "Are you interested? Ha ha!"

That letter plunged me into an intense period of deep soul searching. I walked the streets of Vienna in a daze, praying, thinking, evaluating, and wondering. Why am I even considering making a change? What am I trying to escape from? What would people say? What do I know about youth ministry? What about all the work I had done to get where I am? Finally, I decided that I would apply for the job and would be open to whatever outcome God intended. I kept repeating to myself, "Let go and let God."

So, after a circuitous journey I made the dramatic leap from doctoral candidate and Fulbright scholar to parish youth minister. Instead of thinking about medieval notation, eighteenth-century opera scores, and Baroque cantatas, my mind was on junior high youth group, developing youth leadership, and learning everything I could about a new field. Thankfully, I had wonderful mentors and supportive volunteers to guide me.

I continued to teach music history and piano, simply because I loved it. I thought for some time that I should choose one job, but eventually I realized that, for the sake of my soul, I simply had to do both. I finally had to admit that it wasn't so much a matter of changing horses in the middle of the stream, as it was figuring out a comfortable way to ride two horses.

That realization was a turning point for me; I stopped fighting with myself. The challenges of making both jobs happen were, and continue to be, big ones, though not insurmountable. Two sets of job expectations; two schedules; two bodies of knowledge; two business populations; two sets of working relationships. All in the quest for one authentic life.

EACH OF US WAGES A PRIVATE BATTLE EACH DAY BETWEEN THE GRAND FANTASIES WE HAVE FOR OURSELVES AND WHAT ACTUALLY HAPPENS.

Cathy Guisewite

New Life to Death to New Life

Although I had worked in clinical settings with many who had been diagnosed with depression and shared their struggles with me, I had personally never experienced an extended period of depression until I had a miscarriage. My husband Tom and I had three sons and were open to the possibility of a fourth child in our family. We intentionally sought a pregnancy and felt very much in control of the experience. We were delighted, though not surprised, when it happened.

About twelve weeks into the pregnancy I began to miscarry. It was a devastating blow. I had not experienced complications with any of my previous pregnancies and I believed that miscarriages happened to other people—not to me. With my consent, Tom left on an urgent business trip the day the miscarriage was confirmed. Although saddened about the loss of our baby, Tom did not feel the connection that I had established with the child during the three months that it grew within me. We had not told anyone about the pregnancy yet, so we had no one to share our loss with. I felt as though I knew a wonderful secret that had suddenly faded before my eyes, and now I did not know how to share it with anyone. The unspoken reality of the situation seemed an added burden to me.

I was engulfed with new, foreign feelings. I had little energy, no focus, and I was despondent. I recall thinking, "This must be what depression is like." I struggled for several weeks with intense sadness, despite the efforts of Tom and our three young sons to keep my spirits up. I began to see that I would not be able to simply switch gears and put this behind me. I had hoped that I could work this through by myself, but, realizing that I needed to share this experience with someone, I called the parish office.

A new pastoral minister had recently joined the staff, and I asked if I could come and visit. I had never intentionally sought out professional help other than routine medical care, so this first phone call was a giant hurdle for me. I had to admit that I needed another person to help me through this circumstance in my life.

I was a little hesitant about sharing my deep pain with someone I didn't even know, but I figured it was now or never. The pastoral minister, Joyce, welcomed me into her office and we immediately connected on many levels. We shared stories of our mutual love of the outdoors and our hunting and fishing expeditions. We talked about our shared love of music. On one of her shelves Joyce displayed the very same ceramic statue—a young girl playing a guitar—that my now deceased mother had once given me.

After we established a connection, Joyce invited me to share my story of loss. She listened intently and was totally present to me. She held my hand and cried with me as I shared my experience of letting go of the baby who had become so much a part of me during those months. Through my story, she came to know my family and me. She offered suggestions for ways to ritualize the loss of our child through family prayer and she made sure that when I left her office that day I was given resources that could help me communicate more clearly the intensity and reality of my loss with my family.

Finally, Joyce went to her Bible and retrieved a personal prayer card with hand-written correspondence on the back. On the front, in striking black and white photography, was a picture of an outstretched adult hand reaching for and welcoming a child's hand. She asked me to take the card and remember that I would always be lovingly cared for, just as my baby was being lovingly cared for at that very moment. I returned home determined to bring my husband and young sons more concretely into the experience that I was living.

The family gathered later that week in the living room and lit candles: one candle for each of us and one for our lost child. We shared stories of the excitement that Tom and I felt when discovering each time that we were pregnant and how we felt that all life is a gift from God. The boys shared memories of their siblings' births and early days. I talked about how I had felt during those months, knowing that a new baby was on the way—excited, happy, anxious, thankful. Then I explained how my feelings changed after the miscarriage to sadness, loss, and isolation. We talked about God's plan in our lives and noted that we are not in control. I asked Tom and the boys to pray with and for me as we began to move forward from that day. I also asked them to pray for their sibling, now entrusted to God's eternal care in heaven. We wondered aloud about what his or her name would have been, and I assured our concerned three-year-old son, Jacob, that God would name our baby.

Over time, through repeated conversations with loved ones in my life, I was able to name my feelings and come to own this experience as mine. Through reaching out to others for help and ritualizing this experience of loss with my family at home I began to climb back from the depths of sadness and depression and reach out to the blessings in my life. That beautiful photograph from Joyce still stands on my piano nine years later as a reminder of God's gentle care for our lost baby—and God's care for me through the help of others.

Annmarie and Tom are now the parents of six children—five boys and one girl. Annmarie's painful story of her miscarriage is one that rings true for many women—and men. For her, admitting to the struggle was the beginning of the healing process.

EVEN GOD CANNOT MAKE TWO MOUNTAINS WITHOUT A VALLEY IN BETWEEN.

Gaelic proverb

2

Hold On, Breathe Deeply, and Reach Deep Inside

NO WINTER LASTS FOREVER; NO SPRING
SKIPS ITS TURN.

Hal Borland

Khris was a wonderful young man by anyone's standards. Adults liked him; children liked him; his peers liked him. He was bright, attractive, an "A" student, a natural athlete, a wonderful piano student, deeply spiritual, fun to be around, imaginative, and a thinker. He was in choir, band, and participated in a variety of team sports. He was part of a supportive, loving family and took his role as the oldest of three boys quite seriously. And he was cool; a good, unassuming, natural kind of cool; the kind of cool most of us aspired to be when we were his age.

When I knew Khris he lived in an environment that would challenge even the strongest character, the most confident personality, the most grounded soul: an average American middle school. He told me once that he worried about everything, all the time. He worried about whether he had all his schoolwork done. He always felt like he was forgetting something. Kids in his class mocked him because he liked to sing, and they made fun of him because of his high, prepubescent voice. Although he was good at many different sports, he was short and would likely always be short and he was self-conscious about it.

It was Khris's day for a piano lesson. Due to complicated schedules, I agreed to pick him up from school that day. He got in the car, buckled up, and sighed a huge sigh. When I asked what that was all about, he said that every day before he went to school he looked in the mirror, took a deep breath, and told himself to hold on tight and everything would be okay. When he left school he took another deep breath, grateful that he made it through another day without too much going wrong, and sometimes even had some fun. It was a poignant moment of self-revelation—and a sacred one.

Life is a wild ride for everyone, and we need to hold on tight to all that is good and true inside of us. Each of us is an imperfect creation of a perfect being, and we bring to life the holiness and goodness that is our creator. When we stay true to our own innate goodness and believe that we are indeed holy, we stay grounded in the source of life itself. This sense of being grounded allows us to see adversity for what it is: *part* of the wild ride, not the whole trip.

Taking a deep breath can both prepare us for what is to come and cleanse us from the stress of the day's challenges. Stopping to breathe deeply means the physical action of filling one's lungs to their capacity with air and expelling it slowly; but it also means practicing mindfulness, being aware of all that surrounds us, particularly those things that quiet us. These "deep breaths" are different for each of us, but they have one thing in common: they bring us to a place of peace and remind us to find our inner strength during tough times.

Adversity—whatever form it might take—flows in and out of everyone's life. We cannot eliminate it or control it. However, armed with the expectation that life will be challenging, we can steel ourselves for what is to come, breathe a sigh of relief when it's over, and enjoy most of what comes in between.

> COURAGE IS NOT SIMPLY ONE OF THE VIRTUES, BUT THE FORM OF EVERY VIRTUE AT THE TESTING POINT.
>
> *C. S. Lewis*

Hold On, Breathe Deeply, and Reach Deep Inside

- As you prepare for your day, stand straight and tall, look in the mirror, and stare at your image. Take five deep breaths. Then slowly and deliberately, say the following words: "The 'me' I bring to the world today is strong, courageous, and holy."

- At the end of your day reflect on the following questions:

  - What challenges did I face today?

  - What inner qualities helped me deal with them?

  - What happened that I am most proud of today?

  - What was fun about the day?

- Say a prayer of thanksgiving for whatever goodness made you happy, whatever moments made you proud, and whatever challenges made you stronger.

- We often hear the expression: "I've just got to take a breather." In this expression we indicate our need for a time out of the hassles of life. Evidence shows that even brief rests can dramatically elevate our moods, slow our heart rates, lower our blood pressure, and give us just enough perspective to see things in a fresh light. If we smile while taking a breather, we trigger endorphins— nature's painkillers—that truly do make us feel better. Taking regular time-outs will not necessarily solve a problem, but the practice can give us a momentary retreat before we blow up, tip over into deep sadness, or just throw up our hands.

- Try to find short periods, even three or four minutes, every day to just breathe. Find a comfortable position: many people feel that they can breathe most readily sitting in a straight-backed chair. Then focus your attention on your own breathing. Breathe deeply and slowly so that your inflated lungs push out your abdomen. You can check this by putting your hands on your lower abdomen; feel your breath pushing your hands outward. Listen to your breath coming in slowly and steadily; listen to your breath flowing out. Your in-breaths and out-breaths should take about the same length of time. If thoughts distract you, just let them go and return to listening to your breath. During this time, intentionally smile.

- After focusing on your breathing for a few moments, offer the words of a brief, familiar prayer or quote in harmony with your breathing. The word or words could be a name for God, like, "Come (in-breath), Peace (out-breath)." Or simply say, as Buddhist monk Thich Nhat Hanh teaches, "Calm (in-breath), smile (out-breath)," or "Present moment (in-breath), wonderful moment (out-breath)."

- At the end of your time-out, stand up, stretch, smile, and continue with your daily activities.

OUT OF CLUTTER, FIND SIMPLICITY.

FROM DISCORD, FIND HARMONY.

IN THE MIDDLE OF DIFFICULTY LIES OPPORTUNITY.

Albert Einstein

Facing Puberty and Potty Training—At the Same Time

When the pregnancy test came back positive, I suppose I should have had a more saintly response. After all, I had been a religious educator for most of my adult life. A simple, "Yes, Lord" would have sufficed, but instead I felt a sense of panic and mighty resistance to the news that I was to be a mother again. Rather than saying "let it be done unto me," I prayed for a mistake in the test, a miscarriage; I said a resounding "no" to my own version of the annunciation moment. How could I possibly face

nursing an infant while raising three adolescents? Where
would I find the patience for potty training while
negotiating drivers' training? Just when I thought I had
arrived at the top of the "chutes and ladders" game of
parenting, I hit the big slide and was headed down to the
bottom, having to work my way back up to the freedom of
the post-baby years.

Cursing my conscience that would allow me no other
choice but to bear this new life, I fell into a depression as I
listed every problem imaginable for the next twenty years.
Financially, this pregnancy would be a disaster. Already
working hard to make ends meet, there would be no way
to afford daycare while paying high school and college
tuition. And yet, quitting my job to stay home with the
baby would also derail the education of my older children.
And then there were the layers of guilt that I heaped upon
myself. Beyond the "I should have been more careful"
moments and my "stay-at-home" mom mentality, I felt I
had no right to be upset. My unplanned pregnancy was a
dream situation compared to the nightmare of a teenage
girl, a woman on welfare, or a victim of abuse. How could
I feel so negatively about new life when I had been
preaching a pro-life message for so many years? Now,
having to "walk the talk" seemed like a cruel divine joke.

Yet, it was "the talk" that sustained me. My studies in
theology and scripture at first seemed inadequate as I
worked out my frustrations with God, but slowly the
ancient teachings and passages seeped through my
consciousness to comfort and console me. I had been in
spiritual training for years, and now I was now able to use
strengths that I had built up for such an occasion.

With the help of family and friends, I discovered how
deep the spiritual savings account was. I had a supportive
husband who vowed that we would get through this as we

had other "for better or worse" crises. The excited reaction of my three teenagers both surprised and humbled me. They saw only the good points and none of the disadvantages that concerned me so much.

In the friendships of my community I found lifelines as well. There was the crisis pregnancy volunteer who was willing to open her office late on a Sunday evening to do a free pregnancy test. She spent hours with me, getting me through the initial shock. Colleagues rallied to help create a part-time schedule that would allow me to keep my teaching job with a minimum of time away from my infant.

A friend with whom I walked daily helped me to realize that all the objections and obstacles I posed were surmountable in time. This mother of five reached deep within her own soul to find the words that assured her morning-sick friend that I only had to face each day as it came. Our afternoon walks became symbolic reminders of the need to take one step at a time.

Two other friends, both of whom had lost children, brought the mystery of life into perspective. One friend, whose child had died of multiple birth defects at eighteen months, had also survived a divorce and weathered the agonies of an older son gone astray. I knew that her genuine joy at my news came from the depths of her own experiences of loss and grief. Another wise woman with four older children had intentionally become pregnant in her early forties. When that baby was almost two years old, her fourteen-year-old son was killed in a car accident.

As I struggled to make sense of my own situation, I asked my friend what had possessed her to plan a late in life pregnancy. She sighed deeply as she reflected on how little control we have over life. A split second difference in the sands of time might have prevented her son's death; a different split second leads to new life. The juxtaposition of these two events led her to a deep appreciation of the sacred mystery of life and death. I pondered her words in my heart for a long time.

Ten years after the birth of my son I wonder how or why I ever doubted a wisdom greater than mine. While we may think we can control everything from birth to death, events happen that are not scheduled on the day planners of our lives. What we can control is our response to these events. We have the chance to gracefully live out the problems that come our way. We can move through the suffering, make sense of it, and emerge on the other side grateful and more wise for the experience.

It's amazing how one person's blessing can be another person's crisis. With so many couples facing the excruciating pain of infertility, I wonder what God must think when others find themselves on the "oh, no!" side of a positive pregnancy test. Such was the case with a friend who became pregnant in her early forties—and was already the mother of three teenagers. Her story, in her words, highlights the ability to move from survival to new life.

IF WE'RE TOO INTENT ON

OUR QUESTIONS,

WE CAN'T HEAR GOD'S ANSWERS,

WHICH ARE SURPRISING,

DISCONCERTING,

AND NEVER COME TO US THE WAY

WE EXPECT.

Louis Evely

I Hate Performing

I hate performing. I've been playing the piano for more than forty years, and I've never liked performing for others. I can sing in a chorus with no problem; I can speak in public with little anxiety; but every performance that involves me sitting in front of eighty-eight black and white keys and an audience results in intense stage fright. This is not an uncommon predicament for performers. Many musicians struggle with the same conundrum and use all kinds of techniques to deal with it. They read books, attend seminars, and engage the services of therapists and hypnotists to be able to walk the fine line between productive stress and debilitating angst.

Stage fright did not keep me from performing, mind you. Though I long ago let go of any hopes of a solo career (the great dream of my adolescent years), I periodically found myself in situations where performing was a requirement for whatever I was doing or wanted to do. Most recently, I was invited to be a staff accompanist for vocal students at a university. This meant rehearsing with young singers and coaching them in the finer points of language, musicianship, and period style—all things I loved to do and was good at. However, it also meant accompanying them for recitals and master classes.

Most of the time I was able to keep my stage fright under control, but once in a while I would blow an accompaniment badly and subsequently plunge into a period of doubt, depression, and self-loathing. But a few days later I was back at work and things would go well for a while, until it happened again; and again; and again.

One year I worked with a student who was mature well beyond her age, a wonderful singer, a natural performer, and a pure joy to work with. We were working toward her junior recital at the end of the year. We performed various pieces in various venues all year long. Some went well, some did not. But we made it through. I absolutely loved the music we were doing and I vowed that nothing was going to stop me from making this recital a performance that would be worthy of Libby's gifts, do justice to the repertoire, and demonstrate what I was truly capable of.

The day of the recital finally came. Libby and I were both ready and anxious in a good way. I knew the music completely. I did as much self-preparation as I could possibly do for that night: I prayed, I visualized, I meditated, I did all kinds of self-talk. All in the hopes of conquering my fear and showing our audience what I knew I had inside of me.

Libby's voice teacher also happened to be my best friend, and she more than anyone was aware of my performance struggles. Linell's youngest son was fascinated by the story of the *Three Little Pigs*; his favorite character was the big bad wolf, the "bah bah hof" as two-and-a-half year old Henry called him.

The night of the recital, Linell met Libby and me backstage. After the usual wishes for good luck, she gave me a great big hug and then pulled away, holding her arms apart as if she was taking something with her. She put this imaginary being on the ground and grabbed hold of what I assumed was its hand. As she walked away she told me that she was taking my "bah bah hof " with her. He would sit next to her throughout the evening among the audience of supporters, well-wishers, and music lovers. I watched as Linell walked down the hall, pretending to drag away my personal big bad wolf.

Libby and I made wonderful music together that evening. Every time a wave of anxiety would come over me, I would take a deep breath and think of my big bad wolf sitting in the audience. And I would smile.

I still struggle with stage fright, and if I am called on to perform there's a chance that it will get the best of me. But I know that deep inside I have the power to tame the "bah bah hof" that is bent on blowing my house down, leaving a tattered spirit behind.

COURAGE DOES NOT ALWAYS ROAR. SOMETIMES, IT IS THE QUIET VOICE AT THE END OF THE DAY SAYING, "I WILL TRY AGAIN TOMORROW."

Anonymous

3

Recognize That You've Been There Before

IT IS VITAL TO GIVE YOURSELF CREDIT
FOR THE AGONY YOU HAVE SURVIVED
THROUGHOUT LIFE.

Michael Levine

For most of my life I've lived in cities and metropolitan areas inhabited by at least a quarter of a million people: Buffalo, New York; Los Angeles, California; Vienna, Austria; Cincinnati, Ohio; Dayton, Ohio. Moving to a new location meant learning new routes, names of highways and major streets, and becoming familiar with traffic patterns. Each city has its own traffic personality. As a newcomer to town, my job was to find out what the quirks of that personality were and learn how to deal with them comfortably. After a few months I became quite adept at navigating around my new location. Even Los Angeles, with its freeway system that can only be likened to that of a five-star roller coaster ride at a major amusement park, posed no challenge after a while. I took it all in stride, tattered map in hand, claiming a "parking spot" during my morning commute on the freeway, holding my own, easing in and out of traffic, shifting across five lanes to eventually get to my exit.

However, for about nine years I lived in Winona, a scenic little city perched along the Mississippi River in southeastern Minnesota. Winona cannot exactly be classified as a small town, since it has almost twenty-five thousand people, but since it is not connected to any major metropolitan area it has a small town feel to it. It is a glorious corner of the world.

When I moved to Winona, I had to learn the same things about navigating around the area that I mastered in all the other places I lived. But things were different in Winona; there were a lot fewer routes and highways to memorize. For the most part, the traffic personality of Winona was the same as that of its inhabitants: respectful, careful, and kind. The town is only four-and-a-half miles long and a mile wide and most streets are wide and well maintained. Heavy traffic consists of ten cars lined up at a stop sign. It was a commuter's dream.

One winter afternoon I needed to go downtown. Traffic was brisk as people hurried around to do errands on their lunch hour, and I found myself getting anxious. My eyes darted around nervously, watching for people pulling out of parking spaces, making turns into and out of fast food restaurants, banks, and the post office. As I stopped at a traffic light, it suddenly hit me: Here I was, a person who successfully navigated the busy thoroughfares of southern California for several years, getting tense about driving around friendly downtown Winona. I laughed out loud, almost embarrassed at the realization.

I no longer live in Winona, but I think about that incident almost every time I'm in heavy traffic or on an unfamiliar highway. I have successfully negotiated some of the most brutal traffic in the country and there is no reason why I should not be able to handle whatever comes my way. I'm sure some of those daily drives were tense and slow-going, with more than a few close calls. I know I saw roadblocks, construction, and accidents; and I suppose there were a few times when I sat in gridlock for what seemed like hours; but eventually I made it to wherever I was going.

In many ways, the same holds true for adversity in our lives. We have all survived obstructions and obstacles, dealt with difficult people, and had times when it seemed like we were going nowhere. We find ourselves in the midst of difficult challenges, changes, and crises, only to emerge safely and wiser for the experience. We may need time to brush off our mental self and straighten our emotional clothing after a long, bumpy ride, but we have done it before, and we can do it again.

For example, a person who is grieving a painful loss has likely gone through many other types of loss before. As a child, there could be many tiny losses with the changing of school grade levels and the end of belief in Santa Claus. As a teenager he or she likely endured changes in friendships, the ending of a dream, or graduation from school. As an adult, the person may have dealt with painful endings to relationships, job changes, or empty nest syndrome.

The person who is now despondent over a painful loss can look back at the many different losses in his or her life and be able to say, "I survived those times. I learned many lessons about carrying on. I will survive this time." This does not mean that the grief process will be easier, or shorter, or less painful, but the person can be sure that life will go on.

Each time we successfully navigate a change in life, overcome a difficult challenge, or survive a painful crisis, we learn a little more about ourselves, and we add the experience to our well of remembrance. The more hope we draw from this well, the more history we will add to it. The next time we need to find reassurance in history and hope, this soul-deep well of remembrance is there to be drawn from, again and again.

> What a strange thing is memory, and hope; one looks backward, and the other forward; one is of today, the other of tomorrow. Memory is history recorded in our brain, memory is a painter, it paints pictures of the past and of the day.
>
> *Grandma Moses*

Recognize That You've Been There Before

- Author Patricia Hampl declares, "We only store in memory images of value." Search your memory for instances in which you held on in adversity; even a seemingly small memory can be an "image of value." Write down your memory: who was there, what happened, and how you found your strength. Then pick out one defining moment and write this as a story of overcoming adversity. The next time you need encouragement, pull out this story and read it; then write about another story of overcoming some challenge. Remember: Every incidence of adversity that you have experienced has added something to your well of remembrance.

- Think about the tough times you have dealt with in the last year or so. Find a lidded box or an opaque jar; this will be your well of remembrance. Write each memory down on a piece of paper and deposit it into your jar or box. You may want to decorate your well of remembrance in a way that honors your memories and the lessons you have learned. You will be able to go back to this well of remembrance anytime and gain strength from its contents.

- Think about a struggle that you have recently overcome and the lessons you learned from your experience. You may want to write about your lessons in a journal or put them in a place reserved for your deepest thoughts. Use a formula if you prefer, for example: "My wife and I had an argument about. . . . For the next time, I need to remember that. . . ."

- At the close of each day, take a few moments, sit quietly, and mentally review your day. Note each activity or decision that made a positive impact, even if it is a small one, on the universe. If something happened that you wish had gone better, think about it briefly, then resolve to sleep on it. In the morning see if you have any clarity or new ideas on how to better your future.

I THINK, MYSELF, THAT ONE'S MEMORIES REPRESENT THOSE MOMENTS WHICH, INSIGNIFICANT AS THEY MAY SEEM, NEVERTHELESS REPRESENT THE INNER SELF AND ONESELF AS MOST REALLY ONESELF.

Agatha Christie

A Reluctant Volunteer

I got a call about a month ago from the head office; they are offering me a voluntary retirement package. I am one of many "volunteers" from the company's sales force. They say if they don't get enough volunteers, they will force people to retire. If I take their offer I'll have some money coming in and some benefits, but if I wait and am forced out later, I get nothing. Some choice: little money or no money.

The business world has its own specialized dictionary with its own definitions of words like *volunteer* and *choice* and *retirement*. Most of the people who are being offered this deal have different understandings of those three words also. I'm not even fifty yet. I've got two kids in college and one finishing high school this year. My mom lives with us. My wife works in a parochial school. We're sure not going to survive on her salary alone. I've got to find a way to keep us financially solvent. I simply cannot retire at this point in my life.

This is not the first time I've been "downsized"; it's the third time in twenty years. The first time I was let go I was so upset that I got sick over it and ended up needing surgery. I was eventually rehired by a different division of the same company. I started my new job weak and exhausted from the stress and emotional trauma of being let go.

The second time I wasn't actually let go, but it was a major disappointment in my career. After working hard for eight years to build up my sales territory, my managers asked me to meet them at an airline club in the Boston airport. I thought it was going to be a promotion or at least a change in title to match the level of work I was doing. After all, the company had just done an evaluation of my customers that was very positive. Instead, I was told that my territory was being given to another sales rep with the title I was seeking. I would get a new, smaller territory with fewer customers, but I would still be employed. My immediate supervisor pulled me aside and said quietly "I know you are unhappy, but don't make a big deal over this. Your co-worker coming in after you is being terminated."

I waited in a bar next to the airlines club and saw my colleague walk out after his interview, dejected and demoralized. I didn't have the energy to call out to him. I just couldn't deal with it right then. I had my own pain to deal with. Everything I worked for was gone.

That incident set me back personally and professionally, as once again I found myself face-to-face with an insecure future. I held on to the anger for a long time, and finally had to get therapy to get past it.

And now this. "Voluntary" retirement. I've got to take their offer, but this time things will be a little different. Through the years I've learned a few lessons about coping with the disappointments of corporate life. Some people go through the ups and downs of the business world and handle it badly. They're angry and bitter. They bring everyone else down. I'm screening my calls these days because I just can't listen to some of my peers without becoming angry myself. I just want to get through this with class, honor, and integrity.

I see so many young professionals. I've trained quite a few in my company. They're bright, enthusiastic, creative, and totally committed to their jobs. I want to say to them, "You are bright and gifted. Don't put everything you have into this job. Don't give 200%. Don't burn the candle at both ends. When things get rough in the corporate world—and they most certainly will—your world doesn't have to fall apart. Get a life. Do things that make you happy, things that help you make a difference."

What's next for me? I'm not quite sure, but I've got a little time to explore options. All I know is that I want to do meaningful and productive work. I want to be happy, and I want to continue to provide a good life for my family. I was ordained a deacon in the Catholic church last year; maybe my next move will be deeper into ministry. Maybe I'm being called in some way to help other people who are victims of downsizing. Maybe I'll find another niche in the business world.

I've got a lot to offer the world: experience, wisdom, compassion. Now it's time to get myself going again. I know I can do it.

Tom was employed in corporate sales for almost thirty years. His story of forced retirement is all too common in the business world these days.

IN THREE WORDS I CAN SUM UP
EVERYTHING I'VE LEARNED ABOUT LIFE:
IT GOES ON.

Robert Frost

No Whining

"Mom," my mother announced, "we're broke, and if Jimmy doesn't start making some sales, I don't know what we're going to do. I'm so tired of scraping by." I watched, scared, as tears began to course down my mother's cheeks. My grandmother nodded wordlessly, but her eyes were bright and angry. I knew there would be trouble, because I'd gotten that same look several times right before granny chewed me out.

My grandmother paused. Two of my aunts looked at each other, eyebrows raised as if to say, "Look out. Mom's going to let Helen have it now." I could hear the uncles and my dad slinging bull as they cooked out on the barbecue pit in the back yard. On this hot June Sunday in Tennessee, they would undoubtedly be slaking their thirsts with the Blue Ribbon beer that my Uncle Joe got at wholesale because he delivered it.

Granny cleared her throat. "Helen, tell us about the summer of '35. That was some summer." That's all she said, but recognition moved across my aunts' and mother's faces.

"Ah, Mom, that was a terrible summer. I don't wanna talk about it."

"Tell us, Helen," Granny commanded.

I had heard it all before, though each telling massaged the story this way and that. Given the circumstances this Sunday and who the storyteller was, I listened closely.

"Well, that's the summer I graduated valedictorian from St. Mary's High School," my mother began. Mom had been offered a full scholarship to a local women's college, but that was not to be. The first blow came when my grandfather declared that she couldn't go. His sheet metal roofing business that had boomed in the '20s was now barely able to keep food on the table. Uncle Joe had dropped out of college to work full-time for granddaddy. Uncle Paul and Uncle Louis didn't even bother finishing high school, but were already at work there. My oldest aunt, who we all called Aunt Sister, had married and moved to Detroit where her husband was a reporter for the *Free Press*, but the other aunts all had jobs, contributing what they could to keep the family going.

My granddaddy, now hitting the bottle pretty hard, was none too gentle about telling Mom how silly he thought her dreams of college were. And that was that; she did not go. Mom said that she cried herself to sleep each night. My grandmother tried to console her, as did my aunts. But there just wasn't any money for college.

Now, in the middle of the Depression, Mom spent all day every day for a month trying to find work. She finally lined up a job in a laundry, running a pressing machine. When she came home after the first week and nearly passed out from dehydration, granddaddy made her quit. In another search, she landed a job in the bargain basement of a dime store. Her pay barely covered bus fare, so she walked three miles each way to the store. The work was boring and the customers were tedious. "The only good part about the basement was that it was cool in the summer," she said.

But the summer soon got worse. My Uncle Joe, his friend, two of my aunts, Mom, and Granny took a spin in the friend's new car one Sunday afternoon. They were going to picnic near a lake down in Mississippi. As they careened down a dusty gravel road, a mule wagon rolled out of a field right in front of them. The next any of them knew, the car that had flipped over and they were all crawling out. Everyone except Granny. Aunt Melba had a broken wrist; Mom had sliced open her nose. The others had bumps and bruises, but Granny had broken her back. For months she was bedridden, harnessed into a body cast, waiting to see if she would walk again.

The final blow came late in August. Uncle Paul was everyone's favorite; he was movie star handsome, a superb athlete, clever and witty, and set to take over my grandfather's business in the future. He and his bride of six months radiated love, optimism, and good health. When his tooth began to ache, he ignored it. The business had finally gotten two good contracts and they were trying to finish the roofs on time. By the time he went to the dentist, the infection from the abscessed tooth had spread into his brain. Within days he was dead.

When Mom got to this part of the story, everyone in the room was crying. "Well, Helen," Granny said, "I think the men have finally cooked the ribs. Let's eat. Those kids of yours look hungry."

Granny didn't need to say anything more to Mom. She surely didn't need to remind her that next to the summer of '35, life could only get better. Granny couldn't abide whining, and if anyone started, she only had to ask them about that summer.

A few weeks later, my Mom became the secretary to the president of a university. Even though she was scared—not having worked in many years—she set her face, stuck out her chin, and soon became nearly indispensable. Best of all, the tension between dad and her shrank to a manageable size. They both found ways to look forward, but the change for Mom came from looking back to the summer of '35.

A friend offered this story about his grandmother and mother that illustrates how having a sense of our own history can be a good hedge against tough times.

MEMORY, THAT LIBRARY OF THE SOUL FROM WHICH I WILL DRAW KNOWLEDGE AND EXPERIENCE FOR THE REST OF MY LIFE.

Tove Ditlevsen

4

Honor Your Feelings

THOSE WHO DON'T KNOW HOW TO
WEEP WITH THEIR WHOLE HEART DON'T
KNOW HOW TO LAUGH EITHER.

Golda Meir

My godson Sam and I loved playing with Legos. I would often babysit him when his parents went out for an evening, and I looked forward to any excuse to pull out my collection of brightly colored bricks and build whatever our imaginations sparked that day.

Late one afternoon I picked up Sam from his house and we went by his favorite fast food eatery on our way to an evening of Legos. On the way to dinner he said something that really made me think.

Sam: Marilyn, sometimes when I see you coming, I get very sad.

Me: Why?

Sam: Because I know that mommy and daddy are going away.

He paused for a few seconds, then resumed:

Sam: Marilyn, do you love me?

Me: Yes, I love you *very* much.

Sam: Do you miss me when you don't see me?

Me: Yes, when I don't see you for a long time, I miss you *very* much.

Sam: Well, I don't miss you a lot.

He paused, as if deep in thought.

Nah, I don't miss you at all.

If you know a child well enough, you always know where you stand with him or her. For the most part, children have no trouble expressing their feelings; they may not be able to put exact words to what they feel, but they are able to act on them. They have not yet learned the ways of the world that say that they should keep some feelings to themselves, tame them, or even bury them. It is easy to tell when a child is sad, afraid, delighted, or weary.

There is an irony in it all: One of the tasks of childhood is to learn the words that are associated with the wide variety of feelings and emotions that are part of the human experience. But about the time a child learns to name feelings, he or she enters a world where acknowledging certain emotions is considered a sign of weakness or best expressed in a therapist's office.

I was somewhat surprised by Sam's words, but I recovered quickly and contemplated the implications of our conversation. In the span of a few seconds, Sam acknowledged his feelings of sadness and loneliness when he was separated from his parents, asked for honest feedback about our relationship, and evaluated his emotional attachment to me. This young boy engaged in a process of acknowledging and honoring feelings, which he intrinsically understood as valid and natural. That's quite mature for a six-year-old!

When we live with and through adversity, we often deal with extreme emotions along the way. Feelings of loss, loneliness, anger, frustration, abandonment, and guilt often accompany some of life's most common struggles:

- Ellen spends her days at a job she no longer cares for or about. The management team at the company she works for has changed completely and the corporate philosophy has shifted as well. She feels angry and unappreciated most of the time. And she's stuck. She has two children in high school. Good-paying jobs are hard to find where she lives, and she doesn't want to uproot her children and move.

- Jeff and his wife may as well be separated. They've grown apart. They spend very little time together, and when they do it's only for the sake of appearances. Jeff's wife is well-respected and active in all sorts of church and community organizations. They don't sleep in the same bed and they haven't had a conversation—not even an argument—in weeks. He buries himself in his work so he doesn't have to think about how his marriage is falling apart. He feels abandoned, and the word "lonely" doesn't even begin to describe the depth of his emptiness.

- Cheryl is a member of what's known as the "sandwich" generation. She works forty hours a week. She cares for her elderly mom. Her daughter Alicia is in her twenties and has a history of chemical abuse. Alicia has gone through several jobs and always quits or manages to get fired because of her lifestyle. Alicia had a baby a couple of years ago, and Cheryl often cares for her grandson. At least she is assured that on the days that the little one is with her he is well cared for. Cheryl is exhausted, weary, and sometimes resentful. When she takes time for herself, she feels guilty about it.

Honoring your feelings and emotions is not the same as indulging in self-pity. It is not a sign of weakness or an admission of helplessness. It is an acknowledgment of humanness at its deepest, most fundamental level. Recognizing your feelings of vulnerability and allowing yourself to rely on others is part of what makes us whole, and holy. To honor your own emotions is to show compassion for yourself, which strengthens your compassion for others. To acknowledge your feelings and emotions is to strive for true humility.

In his book *Let Your Life Speak,* Parker Palmer writes about the connection between humility and emotional growth:

> Before spring becomes beautiful, it is ugly, nothing but mud and muck. I love the fact that the word humus—the decayed vegetable matter that feeds plants—comes from the same root that gives rise to the word humility. It helps me understand that the humiliating events of life, the events that leave "mud on my face" or that "make my name mud," may create the fertile soil in which something new can grow.

Recognizing that we sometimes find ourselves deep in the mud and muck of life is as important as acknowledging the mountaintop experiences. We can embrace whatever adversities come our way, because to honor our own feelings is to welcome a chance to grow.

HUMILITY COMES FROM UNDER-
STANDING THAT THE OBSTACLES IN
FRONT OF YOU ARE NOT GOING TO GO
AWAY.

Sarah Ferguson

Honor Your Feelings

- Identify your emotions using a ritual that honors their sacredness. Find a quiet space where you can be alone with your thoughts. Play a recording of soft instrumental music and light a candle. Think about all the emotions that you are experiencing in your current situation. Write each one on a small piece of paper, then place it around the candle. As you do this, repeat a statement like "I acknowledge and honor this feeling of ____. It is a source of growth." You may want to conclude your ritual of emotions with a prayer of thanksgiving for the gift of humanness or a prayer for strength along the journey.

- List in your journal or on a piece of paper all the emotions associated with a particular situation—both those that result in positive feelings and those that are the source of struggle. Describe each one, writing down when you began to feel the emotion and how it impacts your day-to-day living.

- Sometimes we can become so caught up in troubling emotions—sadness, anger, fear, envy—that we miss moments of joy, humor, contentment, and pleasure. All our feelings help balance each other, and by paying special attention to positive emotions we can ease our spirits and edge out the hard emotions that often seem to overwhelm us. Try this exercise to help keep your positive emotions at the forefront of your day:

> On small, colorful slips of paper write prompts such as these—What made you laugh today? Who was kind to you today? When did you take pleasure in something today? Were there any pleasant surprises today? And so on. Place each slip of paper in a pretty bowl, basket or wide-mouth jar. Put your chosen container next to a comfortable chair, or on your bedside table. Each day, sit quietly, read one of the slips, and spend time tapping into your feelings of lightness and hope.

I THINK THAT TIME HEALS *MANY* WOUNDS, BUT OTHERS GET INFECTED. SO THE WISE PERSON WILL TAKE THE TROUBLE TO KEEP THAT WOUND CLEAN AND COVERED FOR A WHILE.

Marilyn vos Savant

I'm Fine. Just Fine.

I had lunch recently with an old friend—a religious sister—brimming with wisdom. Not the kind of wisdom that comes from studying theology or spending years behind convent walls, but the kind that comes from living in this world as a teacher, missionary, and parish minister. No stranger to adversity, she has encountered both the agony and the ecstasy of a life well lived.

On this particular day, we met because she was leaving our faith community to rejoin her community of Sisters at the motherhouse. As we sat to dine on Mexican food and delight in each other's company, I asked her how she was. Her immediate reply was, "I'm sad. But that's okay, because I am supposed to be sad. A year ago, if you asked me how I was, I would have said, 'I'm fine,' even though I was anything but."

What changed for this wise woman? She spent six months in treatment for alcoholism. In treatment she learned that her trigger response of "I'm fine" was a defense mechanism to hide the truth about her addiction not only from others, but from herself.

Her parents had both been alcoholics—it was one of those family secrets that was never talked about. Knowing the toll it had taken on her family, she convinced herself that it would never happen to her. She entered the convent in her late teens during an age of innocence that had culturally sheltered her from drugs or alcohol. She hoped that her vocation would protect her from the addiction. And it did for a while.

After a brief teaching career and several overseas missionary assignments, the opportunity surfaced to minister in a city far away from her community. The work was good, she was needed there, and her community agreed to let her go. Her ministry at the city's parish led to wonderful friendships with families, single and divorced women, and gay and straight couples. Much of her social life revolved around meals and celebrations where the wine flowed as freely as the conversations.

Over the years, Sister began to notice that her drinking was becoming a problem. One glass led to two, and then maybe three or four. But alcoholism is an addiction that is easy to deny—*especially* if you're a nun. After all, nuns just aren't drunks. At one point, Sister confided to one of her closest friends in the community that she felt she needed to quit. At her friend's encouragement, she joined an Alcoholics Anonymous chapter, but embarrassment and fear that she might see someone she knew kept her from regular attendance. Besides, she never believed that her problem was that bad.

As the years went on, Sister kept herself busy and overwhelmed, good distractions that masked her reality. Instead of getting better, her untreated addiction only became worse. Her close friend from her community would occasionally call or see her and cryptically ask how she was. The stock response, of "Fine, just fine" kept the inquisitor at bay. But time and the bottle were making their mark, and ten years after her initial admission, her confidante saw her at a conference and was shocked by Sister's appearance. The "I'm fine" mask had started to crack.

Within a few weeks, her good friend and fellow nun had the wheels turning toward an intervention. Sister was called back to the motherhouse and confronted by her superiors. Still not believing that she really needed help, she entered rehab for evaluation, not planning to stay.

Now at our lunch together six months later, Sister was able to name her demons. She commented that alcoholism is like a disease—only worse. When someone has cancer, there is great sympathy. Friends and family rally round in support. But addictions carry the burden of shame and weakness, of some*one*—not some*thing*—gone wrong.

Yet another feeling had surfaced as she remembered those initial days in rehab. It was relief. Relief that she was finally getting help and that she did not have to face her addiction alone. She said that her life without alcohol was a life of great hope.

As we parted ways, I felt humbled by her story. But I also thought to myself that my friend was no longer in hiding. She was, at last, "just fine."

COMPASSION   DIRECTED   TOWARD
ONESELF IS HUMILITY.

Simone Weil

A Familiar Grief

I hadn't expected the emotions I experienced when my dog, Nicholas, died. We had been together for fourteen years and he was the most constant source of love in my adult life. I never took for granted how lucky I was to "own" Nicholas, but I was totally unprepared for the suddenness of his death, and for the strength and familiarity of my grief.

The veterinarian said Nicholas had "kennel cough," the canine equivalent of a very bad cold. I wanted to believe her. Eventually, his cough dissipated, but he was slowly losing the effervescent spirit that had always been his hallmark. I took him back to the vet in hopes of finding a cure for his recent lethargy.

I was stunned when X-rays showed Nicholas's lungs to be filled with cancer. The doctor was only able to give me the results of the tests before I silently, uncontrollably dissolved into tears. I cried for the next seven days. The day after the diagnosis, Nicholas lay in my arms as the doctor injected him with the sleep he now welcomed. He took only seconds to drift away.

I realize now that Nicholas said his good-byes to me that day in the car on the way to the vet's office. As he had when he was a puppy, he lay calmly on the seat beside me, but kept nuzzling my hand, demanding that I continuously pet his head as I drove. Each time I removed my hand to shift gears, he would push his nose up to remind me to return to the petting position as soon as possible.

I always appreciated how much love and joy Nicholas added to my life, but he was my pet, my dog, an animal, and somehow I expected my sorrow when I lost him to be different from that of losing a person. As if we humans have a separate set of feelings and emotions for animals than those we feel for people. I was unprepared to recognize the face of this grief so completely.

I recognized the anguish of looking forward to going home to see him, and then suddenly remembering that he wouldn't be there. I recognized the loneliness when I longed to hug the loved one who had disappeared. I recognized the frightening feeling of being so much more alone in the world than I had been before. And I recognized my self-pity over losing one who loved me.

I knew there would be those who could not understand the depth of my grief over a dog. Anyone who has ever loved a pet has at one time or another felt a bit embarrassed when a non-pet owner scoffs, "It's just an animal." But I felt the pain nonetheless.

What value is there in the love of an animal? Pets bestow the rarest of all gifts—unconditional love. We humans try our best to love unconditionally. We promise in songs, poetry, and vows to love one another forever. But despite our best intentions we eventually fall short of that promise. Our egos get in the way of giving truly unconditional love. Our self-esteem is too easily threatened by change. When our loved one has a bad day and takes it out on us, we take it personally. If our partner needs time alone, we fear abandonment.

Animals do not suffer from ego. They love our truest self, that core part of our being whose essence does not change from cradle to grave. When we suffer anxiety over our own self-worth, animals challenge us to accept our own goodness, and reassure us that we are lovable. They allow us to grow and change without fear of losing their love.

Perhaps we consider human love to be more valuable than animal love because of all we have to overcome to give and receive it. That people love one another despite the difficulties of overcoming ego is amazing. People choose to love. When they choose to love us, we feel the miracle. Pets love us unconditionally and forever because of our core goodness. Humans choose to love us despite our faults. What incredible gifts!

Nicholas taught me invaluable lessons about love and sorrow. I hope I leave as rich a legacy to those I love.

Even those who have never lost a pet can relate to this story from Alice. For most of us, our pets are the only creatures that love us in spite of ourselves. Yet we are often reluctant—and even ashamed—to admit to our grief when that animal is no longer part of daily life.

HE WHO HAS NO TIME TO MOURN HAS NO TIME TO MEND.

John Donne

5

Remember That You're Not Alone

TO CHERISH SECRETS AND HOLD BACK
EMOTIONS IS A PSYCHIC MISDEMEANOR
FOR WHICH NATURE FINALLY VISITS US
WITH SICKNESS.

Carl Jung

The show *Queen for a Day* was a popular program in the early days of television. Female contestants would vie for the title of queen by telling their sad story to the studio audience. After all the women had poured out their stories, the audience would vote via an applause meter for the saddest story of all. The one who generated the most applause would be crowned "queen for a day." She was clothed in a velvet robe, crowned, and then walked down the studio runway to the tune of *Pomp and Circumstance*. Amid the sobs, the queen would learn that she had won a washer and dryer, refrigerator, or another gleaming appliance because she had elicited the most sympathy from others. The losers' lives became that much more grim since they walked away with nothing.

Many of today's talk shows and live courtroom sessions fill the void left by this popular but insensitive "game show" from the 1950s. There is always someone who is willing to sell their troubles for fifteen minutes of fame, and more than a few people who have at least a passing interest in the misfortune of others. Perhaps we tune in to such shows because we take some comfort in knowing that others are worse off than we are. Or maybe we just like to know that other people struggle with the same problems we do.

In his book *All Grown Up and No Place to Go,* Dr. David Elkind describes the myth of the "personal fable" that is characteristic of young teenagers. They live with the illusion that no one is like them. No one has the same feelings or the same experiences that they do. Thus, they keep their struggles to themselves, convinced that sharing their tough times would mark them for life as different from everyone else.

Many years ago I was leading a junior high youth group meeting on the topic of dealing with tough times. The group was made up of about thirty-five teenagers in grades six, seven, and eight. In one exercise they had to look over a list of situations and mark the ones that they worried about. The list included things like what high school would be like, death of a parent, getting a good job when they grew up, and making friends—all common concerns for young teens. After they completed the list, I asked them to write their top three worries on a small piece of paper. We then compiled the results of these thirty-five anonymous admissions of struggle.

I will never forget the shocked look on one boy's face when he realized that eight other people in the group had named "I have a parent who drinks too much" as one of their top three struggles. For James, a quiet, thoughtful seventh grader, it was the beginning of an understanding that he was not alone in his struggle. His family wasn't unique, and his concerns were valid. At that moment, James' sense of "personal fable" had developed a liberating crack in it.

To some extent, we still hold on to the myth of the personal fable as adults. We are reluctant to share the tough times in our lives with those closest to us, perhaps out of embarrassment or a sense of failure. But the fact is that adversity is a universal experience. It is one of the things that unites us as creatures who share life on this planet.

In preparation for this book I invited friends and relatives from all around the country to share their stories of adversity. I was struck by the thematic consistency of people's stories, which revolved around issues like these:

- The feeling of failure when a child does not live up to expectations or when a teenager gets into serious trouble;

- The frustration and fear that is often part of the process of conceiving, birthing, or adopting a child;

- The challenge of being a caregiver and the emotional roller coaster that is part of the job;

- The pain of feeling personally defective or flawed;

- The reassessment of priorities and recognition of the presence of the creator in a time of personal illness or when a family member is sick;

- The sense of inadequacy that accompanies news of a job loss;

- The disillusionment when significant relationships fall apart;

- The embarrassment when a relative is in trouble with the law;

- The panic that comes with a financial crisis and the fear that the family will not be taken care of.

I suspect that the issues the people I know deal with are the same issues that cause most of us to lose sleep. We hate to admit that our life is less than perfect, because we're pretty sure that everyone else's life is spectacularly flawless. The fact is that many people deal with the same struggles as we do. We each approach them differently and respond uniquely, but at the core the struggle is the same. This notion is borne out by the number of people in support groups and twelve-step programs who are there because they have something in common.

Understanding that other people worry, feel inadequate, get embarrassed, experience fear, and operate from day to day in less than ideal conditions can be liberating, especially if we are willing to listen to their stories and tell our own. When we let go of our personal fable and are open to the possibility of disclosing our concerns to others, what may have seemed like our own private hell becomes a shared journey toward wholeness.

REALITY IS THE LEADING CAUSE OF STRESS AMONG THOSE WHO ARE IN TOUCH WITH REALITY.

C. Everett Koop

Remember That You're Not Alone

- Write your own "personal fable" in the form of lists: that is, list all of your secret worries, fears, doubts, hates, and anything about which you feel shame. Here are some starters to use; for each one list all of your responses:
  - Worries that steadily bother me . . .
  - Things that make me fearful on a regular basis are . . .
  - I am deeply ashamed of . . .
  - People would think I'm weird if they knew I . . .
  - Deep inside me, I am really angry about . . .

- Our "personal fable" many times also contains aspects of our lives about which we feel very positive, but we hide them from others because we are fearful of their rejection. List your secret wishes and joys using prompts like these:
  - If I felt freer, I would like to . . .
  - I take silent pleasure in these aspects of who I am . . .
  - I wish that I could . . .
  - I receive great satisfaction in . . .
  - People I really enjoy and like to be with include . . .

- Write a "letter" to your shadows: those parts of yourself which you try to hide or that conflict with the way you want to be seen. First, greet the shadows and then tell the shadows what you know and understand about them. Tell your shadows why you keep them hidden away.

- On the back of the page write a letter back to yourself from your shadows. Let the shadows speak about what they do to you to keep them hidden and have them suggest people who could help you deal with them.

- Write a note to someone you know who is dealing with a difficult situation similar to one you've dealt with before. Offer your support and reassurance, and invite him or her to meet with you for coffee and conversation.

- The next time you feel alone in adversity make a mental list of all the people you know who have faced or are facing similar difficulties. For example, if you are parenting a troubled teen, list all the parents you know who are facing comparable situations. You may want to list these people in a journal and refer to it periodically, offering a prayer that they may successfully navigate the parenting waters.

- If you feel comfortable doing so, try starting a group for people dealing with similar issues to offer support to one another. Or you may want to talk with a leader in your faith community about sponsoring such a gathering.

- In the movie *Shadowlands,* about the writer C. S. Lewis, one of Lewis's former students tells him that he reads so that he does not feel so completely alone. If you feel alone, go to a bookstore or library and search for books on a secret you find it impossible to talk about. There are many books in which people share their stories—stories that you might have written yourself. Pick one or two books; see how the writers dealt with secrets similar to yours. Even if their approach won't work for you, at least you will know that you are not alone in the universe.

THERE IS NO SHORTAGE OF GOOD DAYS.
IT IS GOOD LIVES THAT ARE HARD TO
COME BY.

Annie Dillard

Make That Thirty

It was a typical parent group on a typical evening in a typical high school in a typical American suburb. I was there to do a presentation for parents on suicide prevention and teenagers. As a trained volunteer speaker with the adolescent outreach group of the county suicide prevention center, I visited dozens of middle school and high school classrooms each year, talking to teens about depression and how to reach out for help. We talk about recognizing the signs that a friend might be suicidal and what to do if they think someone they know is headed for trouble. I tell them that having feelings of depression and thoughts of suicide are more common among their peers than they might think.

I give statistics like, "There are 346 sophomores at Central High. About thirty-five of those 346 will attempt suicide before they reach the age of eighteen. Some of them won't graduate for that reason." I could see the young people looking rather horrified at the thought. And when I told them that of those 346 sophomores, at least half have or will have thoughts about suicide, their quick glances told me that quite a few of them identified strongly with that statistic. By the end of the presentation, there was a quiet calmness in the group, the kind that comes with knowing that you are in solidarity with people who feel the way you do, who are in pain, who struggle, and who triumph.

On this particular evening I was talking to a group of sixty parents about the same issues: the differences between a bad day and depression, the suicidal process, statistics, and recognizing the signs of these troubles in their teenager. They listened carefully, asking clarifying questions and telling stories—mostly about *other* people's children. Suicide in one's own family is not a topic that is easily shared in public.

One exercise brought a sense of quiet unity to the group. I asked them to close their eyes and cover them with one hand so that they were sure they could not see anyone. Then I asked them to put their free hand over their heart if they remember seriously thinking that suicide might be an option during a difficult time in their life, whether it was as a teenager or as an adult. Hands began to move up—slowly, cautiously, silently. Some people hesitated, thinking hard about the well-kept secret they were about to reveal.

After what I'm sure seemed like an eternity to some people, I asked them to put their hands in their lap and open their eyes. I revealed to them that twenty-nine people had put their hand over their heart, indicating that they had thought about suicide. The group first expressed shock and disbelief that such thoughts were common. But one particularly courageous person, a dad in his early forties, announced that he was relieved. Richard told this story about his junior year in college.

> I was twenty-one. I had a tough academic load and worked a couple of part-time jobs. My girlfriend of two years had recently given me the "I just want to be friends" speech. My dad lost his factory job because the company went bankrupt. He found out about it the week after we buried his mother. My grades were falling; I didn't want to go out or be with my friends; I didn't care much about anything or anyone. I just wanted out.
>
> Every fall my brothers, my dad, and I went hunting at a farm over a weekend. Though I always looked forward to the trip, I didn't want to go that year. But I knew better than to interfere with this annual family ritual. Besides, I thought I had the perfect solution to my problems. I could kill myself easily and make it look like an accidental self-inflicted gunshot wound. We wouldn't stay together the whole time, though we were always within shouting distance. So I went through the motions of preparing for the trip, feigning excitement for my dad's sake, and making plans for my "accident."
>
> When we arrived at the farm everyone started setting up his own tree stand. My dad came over to me. "Do you need help?" he said. "It looks like you're having some trouble here. Did you forget how to set one of these things up?" I looked at my father and said "Yeah, I think I need some help." My dad—not someone given to emotional

displays or talk about feelings—launched into a discourse about the finer points of setting up a tree stand. Then he looked at me and said "You know son, there's nothing like some time away with people you care about to make you think twice about the things that are important in this life." I didn't know if my dad was speaking to me, aware of my struggles, or if he was talking about himself, a recently unemployed factory worker with a family to support who had just lost his mother. But it didn't matter. I knew at that moment that I could not go through with my planned "accident."

No one got a deer that year. We went back home, unpacked, and went about our daily lives. Eventually, things fell into place for me. I never told anyone about my plan, nor did anyone ever ask. I guess I've been too ashamed to tell anyone that I got to that point.

When Richard finished his story, the room was quiet. I thanked him and noted that it might be comforting for some to know that twenty-nine people in this room have something in common—emotional pain that resulted in thoughts of suicide. I was about to move on to the next part of the evening when a woman at the back of the room raised her hand. She stood up slowly, said in a loud and clear voice, "Make that thirty," and sat back down. As she did so, I thought I heard a deep, cleansing sigh coming from where she sat.

THE FACT THAT WE ARE HUMAN BEINGS IS
INFINITELY MORE IMPORTANT THAN ALL
THE PECULIARITIES THAT DISTINGUISH
HUMAN BEINGS FROM ONE ANOTHER.

Simone de Beauvoir

Tragedy and Hope in the ICU

At age seven, my daughter Kristen was a whirlwind of energy: unstoppable, inquisitive, fun-loving, and the picture of health. Even though she complained of a sore throat at a Fourth of July celebration, Kristen didn't miss a beat, insisting on racing with her cousins and reveling in the fireworks. A trip to the doctor's the next morning resulted in a course of antibiotics with the expectation that all would be better in a day or two.

Roger and I never expected the roller coaster we encountered in the following days. Kristen's condition deteriorated, and we placed another call to the pediatrician's office. He ordered some lab work, which we had done immediately. However, the results didn't get back to him until it was almost too late.

Three days later Kristen became lethargic and sick to her stomach. She didn't sleep all night, and neither did I. At dawn I called the pediatrician again. He, too, was worried and suggested we take Kristen to a local hospital immediately. At the hospital, Kristen developed seizures and became weaker. As the hours wore on and it became apparent that Kristen was not responding to treatment, the medical staff talked to us about transferring Kristen to Children's Hospital. Her condition was deteriorating quickly, and I requested that the Catholic chaplain give her last rites.

Nothing prepares a mother for the sight of her desperately ill child receiving this sacrament. Although I felt helpless dealing with the medical procedures at this point, I gathered strength from the words of the priest and knew that I could request prayers for Kristen from friends and family. We were not alone in our hour of need, and the flood of prayers began.

By the time the doctors at Children's Hospital examined Kristen, she was in a coma. They determined that her kidneys were failing, and she was unable to filter poisons from her system. The doctor took us into a small room and informed us that Kristen's potassium levels were sky high. He said that he had never seen anyone survive such an extreme level. At that point I fell to my knees and prayed from the depths of my soul.

Kristen was placed in intensive care where she was monitored in the event of a heart attack. Her blood pressure shot up and they prepared her for kidney dialysis. The doctors feared brain damage as evidenced by the seizures. All we could do was pray and wait.

There were thirteen beds in the solemn, dimly lit intensive care unit, and families were allowed to be with their loved ones for limited amounts of time. The close proximity of the patients and the families huddling in the waiting room drew us all together. As the days wore on we shared the sorrows, joys, and prayers of twelve other families. We were a community joined together by tragedy, by fear, and by hope. We shared news of our children's progress or setbacks. We prayed with and for each other. I'm sure not everyone in the ICU was of the same religion, but at that moment we were all people of faith. And nothing else mattered.

Kristen remained in a coma for three days. Finally her condition was stabilized, and the doctors became cautiously optimistic. It was a great moment for us all when she was removed from the ventilator; after that she slowly regained consciousness and came back "to life."

Kristen had no memory of being ill and was puzzled when she woke up in a hospital. Miraculously she picked up where she left off as a bright-eyed seven-year-old, curious about her new surroundings. To Kristen, the hospital was a fun place with games, new people, and lots of attention. Kristen's recovery was not immediate, but eventually she was returned to perfect health, with no permanent damage.

Twelve years have passed since that crisis, though I recall every moment vividly. Yes, there was the terror and uncertainty, but there was also a great lesson I learned from this event. In the midst of my busy life, often on a sunny day, I think of that dimly lit intensive care ward with thirteen beds holding thirteen young lives. I say a prayer for them and the hospital staff and a prayer of thanks for the people that prayed for and cared for Kristen. And I say a prayer for the parents of the twelve children in the ICU with Kristen. We share a special bond with each other and with millions of other parents who have gone through the hellish experience of almost losing a child. I hope they know that they are not alone.

Joan and Roger live in western New York with their two daughters and two cats. Kristen has grown into a fun-loving college student who does volunteer work in the same hospital where she was a patient.

THE PERSONAL, IF IT IS DEEP ENOUGH,
BECOMES   UNIVERSAL,   MYTHICAL,
SYMBOLIC.

Anaïs Nin

6

Develop a Network of Care

CALL IT A CLAN, CALL IT A NETWORK, CALL IT A TRIBE, CALL IT A FAMILY. WHATEVER YOU CALL IT, WHOEVER YOU ARE, YOU NEED ONE.

Jane Howard

I looked forward to the picnic we had planned for late Friday afternoon. It had been a tough week: a deadline at work, a confrontation with a colleague, a forgotten appointment that I would have to pay for anyway, yet another delay by the contractor who was doing some repairs on my house, some family issues, too much to do in too little time. It was the type of week that makes one heave a sigh of relief when it's finally over, grateful that no major meltdown occurred. So when Friday came I eagerly anticipated spending some time with my friend and her two young children.

It was early summer. We planned to meet at a local park for a picnic supper and some hiking in the bluffs that were teeming with new life. The dramatic change that occurred in those bluffs every year always reminded me of the miracle of creation and re-creation. I drove to the park looking for my friend and her children, finally spotting them at the top of a hill where they had set up our picnic. About the same time, seven-year-old Esther and four-year-old Henry saw my tan Honda Civic and raced down the hill to greet me. I heard them calling "Fafa," the nickname bestowed upon me by Henry when he was just learning to talk. Though it was no longer necessary, the moniker stuck and was used by both children. When they got to the car I showed them what I had brought for our picnic and asked if they would help me carry things. They each took something and we started up the hill. As we did so, Esther took my hand and said to me "Hold my hand, Fafa. It's a long way up the hill, and it's very steep."

At that moment my eyes filled with unexpected tears. Esther could not possibly have had any idea how steep my hill had been that week, nor how endless the trek seemed. Yet, this innocent act by my little seven-year-old friend was balm for my battered spirit. I walked with the children, silently trying to compose myself, listening to stories of their day and their plans for our time together.

As much as we'd like to think otherwise, none of us can handle the adversities of life alone. Nor were we meant to. We are born into a community we call family, and hopefully our birth was the result of a love story between two members of that community. We spend our early years learning to be social. We learn to interact with others and the basic rules of relationships. During our school years we explore different options for community that go beyond the immediate family. We form friendships based on common interests. During adolescence our friendships deepen as we look for people with whom we could be ourselves. As young adults we go in search of soul-mates with whom we can be spiritually, emotionally, intellectually, and perhaps physically intimate. The whole point of the process is to have people to share life with. All of life. The clouds and the silver linings. For richer, for poorer, in sickness, and in health. The good, the bad, and the ugly.

Finding a network of care means tapping into a community of people whose lives intersect with our own and who have expressed a willingness to walk the journey with us and be present to our spirit. It requires one thing on our part: a willingness to take an emotional risk. Unfortunately when times get tough we often withdraw within the walls of secrecy, sometimes out of embarrassment, sometimes out of pain. We fail to tap into the network of care that could be a source of support for us, cushioning our falls and providing balm for our battered spirit.

Based on her I.Q. score, Marilyn vos Savant is purported to be the most intellectually gifted person in America. She writes a column that appears in many newspapers across the country. Among the mind-bending puzzle challenges, queries about how things work, and social commentary, she frequently offers musings about the human condition. One question asked about the difference between a broken heart and a broken spirit, to which vos Savant offered this piece of wisdom about building a network of care:

> The major difference between a broken heart and a broken spirit is that people break hearts and time mends them, but *time* breaks spirits and *people* mend them. My suggestion is that you take any broken spirit you know and expose it

repeatedly to the light of as many warm personalities as possible.

Developing a network of care means surrounding yourself with people who will notice and tend to your broken spirit, and expect that you will do the same for them. They are people who recognize that their need is the same as yours: for companions on the journey toward wholeness. Age is not important, and they need not be a relative. These are people who by their very presence in your life reach out with the message that Esther offered me that summer afternoon: "Hold my hand, Fafa. It's a long way up the hill, and it's very steep."

THE ONLY ANSWER IN THIS LIFE, TO THE
LONELINESS WE ARE ALL BOUND TO
FEEL, IS COMMUNITY.

Dorothy Day

Develop a Network of Care

- Consider these questions. You may want to write your answers in a journal or another safe place.

  - Think about all the formal and informal communities you are part of: family, friends, work group, sports team, professional organization, parent association, special interest club, and so forth. Who from these communities is or could be part of your network of care?

- When have you been part of someone else's network of care? What was that experience like?

- Describe a time when you were reluctant to reach out for support because of embarrassment, fear, or simply the depth of your pain. Describe a time when you reached out in spite of your hesitation. What was the impact of each situation on your spirit?

- Draw four concentric circles. Write your name in the center circle. In the outermost circle, list the communities you belong to. In the next circle list the names of people in those communities to whom you feel particularly close. In the circle closest to you write the names of the people who would most likely be part of your network of care: that is, the people you would be most likely to reach out to when things are tough.

- The organization known as the *Syracuse Cultural Workers* publishes a poster entitled "How to Build Community." It lists ways to bring people together to create the type of neighborhood community that can evolve into a network of care for residents of the area. You can purchase a copy of the poster, note cards, or bookmarks by logging on to www.syrculturalworkers.com.

- Decorate the outside of an empty jar or can with words and pictures that describe what a network of care means to you. Each day, write one person's name on a slip of paper and think about why you consider that person to be part of your network, then add it to the jar or can. Do this until you run out of names. Periodically look over the names in your jar, especially when you are struggling.

EVERYTHING BECOMES A LITTLE
DIFFERENT AS SOON AS IT IS SPOKEN
OUT LOUD.

Hermann Hesse

Hoping for a Miracle

Almost fifteen years into her marriage to Bud, Mary was living a typical middle-class life with their three boys ranging in age from preschooler to preteen. They had chosen to live a simple life in a small town. She was a nurse; he worked for a trucking company. Then Bud lost his job. Months went by with no prospects, and he slipped into a troubling, but familiar, depression. A Vietnam vet, he didn't talk much during these times, but a simmering anger boiled over into bursts of violence that frightened and dismayed his wife.

However, nothing could have prepared Mary for her husband's desperate attempt to provide for his family. She was at work at the hospital when she learned that Bud had just been arrested for armed robbery. There was no question about his guilt. The police were waiting for him as he drove into the driveway in the family station wagon. The money was stowed in the back where book bags and soccer balls belonged.

The early days were the toughest, as Mary faced an unrelenting media, her husband's mug shot on the front page of the local newspaper, and hardest of all, her boys' questions about their daddy. Her private life had suddenly become a public humiliation. Her first thought was to run and hide, change her name, and move away, so she would not have to deal with friends, neighbors, and colleagues, let alone the multitudes of strangers who knew the story. But with only one income now and legal bills, she elected to stay, trying to keep her home and family intact. Besides, she would be close enough to visit Bud who awaited trial without bond.

Staying in town proved a good decision. Rather than isolation from her community, Mary found support and friendship. As neighbors reached out to her with food, babysitting offers, and emotional handholding, she found that she could survive day by day. She experienced a spiritual conversion and lived a life of prayer. The words she found within the pages of her Bible touched her soul and gave her a sense of hope when the circumstances of her life dictated nothing but despair.

Months passed. The long awaited trial date arrived, but the defense lawyers were frustratingly disinterested. Still, Mary hoped that with no prior record and pages of character references, Bud's sentence would be light.

She was devastated when he was sentenced to fifty years to be served at a prison hundreds of miles away. In his early forties, Bud began what appeared to be a life sentence. Mary felt imprisoned as well by her life as a single mother. She was overwhelmed by her job, her children, and bills that were well beyond her ability to pay. But her prayer life and the consistent support from her community kept her sane and focused.

Disregarding the suggestions that she might be better off divorced, she wrote nightly letters to her husband, lacing her epistles with the words of Scripture. Convinced that she could pray Bud out of prison, she refused to give up hope while others shook their heads at her quixotic efforts to plead her husband's case with anyone who could help. She badgered judges and called on lifelong family friends and complete strangers for legal advice.

Mary tried to balance the needs of her children and the demands of her nursing career with her crusade to help Bud. Always a nurturer, Mary's compassion for others intensified. One of her patients was a woman with terminal cancer. Mary became her full-time nurse, ministering to her and to her husband, who kept a constant vigil. Mary was part of their network of care. After his wife's death, the man wanted to repay the kindness that Mary had shown to them during the last days of her patient's life. When he learned of Mary's personal misfortune, he came to her with an offer she couldn't refuse. He was a well-respected and successful lawyer who would take her husband's appeal on a pro bono basis.

Within a year Bud was back in court with his new lawyer, asking for a new trial on the grounds that the legal team in his first trial operated under a blatant conflict of interest. After reviewing the case, the judge's decision surprised almost everyone. He ordered Bud to be released immediately, with the stipulation that if he would stay clean for ten years all records of his incarceration would be expunged. As the chains of his shackles fell to the floor in the courtroom, Mary stepped forward with a small suitcase packed with street clothes for Bud, a sign of her hope that he would come home that day.

Given a new lease on life, Bud sought the help he had needed for years by checking himself into a veterans' hospital for treatment of post-traumatic stress syndrome. Ten years after the whole ordeal began, Mary and Bud celebrated quietly the miracle of true freedom.

Throughout their ordeal, Mary resisted the temptation to flee into the shell that seemed to beckon her on a daily basis. Instead, she availed herself of any and all offers of help. Mary's openness to human and divine intervention made a difference in the face of tragedy.

Mary's remarkable story of living through adversity is a story of hope, commitment, faith, and of a symbiotic network of care that eventually resulted in what some would call a miracle.

THE HEARTS THAT NEVER LEAN, MUST FALL.

Emily Dickinson

You Are My Sunshine

When my husband and I bought our house, we considered the possibility that someday we would have either Mama or my sister, Liz, come and live with us. Never in a million years did we figure on getting them both! But splitting them up was not an option. Mama and Liz had been together since the day Elizabeth was born thirty-seven years ago. The sixth of seven children, Liz was born with Down's syndrome and was not expected to live past the age of two. It was God's grace and Mama's care that kept her alive and growing. They always had a special bond, one that was never meant to be broken.

Ray and I lived about seventy-five miles away from Mama and Liz. We visited frequently and checked in all the time. Mama was becoming more and more forgetful and confused as the days went on. She forgot medications or overmedicated. She could no longer drive. She forgot food cooking on the stove. She cried constantly. I worried constantly.

It was apparent that she could no longer live by herself and care for Elizabeth. The signs all pointed to Alzheimer's disease. I asked her if she would rather have someone come and live with her or if she would like to move in with us. She answered hopefully, "Can we come and live with you?" I called my husband and told him the news. He was not surprised, since we had discussed this possibility between us and with our two sons, the youngest of whom still lived at home. When he answered the phone I said, "Ray, rent the truck." His only response was, "Are you sure?" I assured him that this was the only workable solution. He immediately got on the phone to the local U-Haul agent.

When I told one of my friends at work about Ray's response to the impending change in our lives she commented, "My husband would not allow that!" I looked at her sadly and thought to myself, "Girlfriend, you married the wrong kind of guy!"

The first year was an adjustment for us all, although I think Mama and Liz adjusted more quickly than I had imagined they would. They were safe and happy. Elizabeth did well in her new program for developmentally challenged adults. Mama continued to decline, as Alzheimer's patients do, but she was content to be with Elizabeth, her anchor. I can still remember Mama singing

Elizabeth to sleep every night. Even though Liz was thirty-seven, she was still a young child in so many ways. Mama liked to sing the song "You Are My Sunshine," and it brings tears to my eyes whenever I hear it.

I finally had the mother I never had growing up, the one I always wanted. My old mother was from the Old World. The oldest daughter of poor Polish immigrants, she never displayed affection. Her philosophy toward parenting was, "I'm here and taking care of you, aren't I? That must mean I love you. Now get out of here and leave me alone." My new mother thought I was the greatest thing since sliced bread! She kissed me and thanked me every day. She hummed. She prayed. She washed the dishes constantly. Elizabeth, realizing in her own way that our mother was losing ground, became quite attached to me as well as Mama. Their faces lit up when I entered the room. It was a wonderful feeling to be so loved.

Mama knew she was forgetting more and more each day. Countless times she asked me hopefully, "You won't put me in the loony bin, will you?" I assured her over and over that she would stay with us, that this is where she belonged, and that we could take care of her.

Elizabeth's health declined. Her heart was wearing down, a common occurrence for people with Down's syndrome. Mama's angel, her anchor, her reason for holding on to her own life, died two years after coming to live with us. Mama declined rapidly after that. The last months of her life were the hardest for all of us. She was already in her own little world, and watching her deteriorate was excruciatingly painful. At the end we could only keep her safe, and that gave us peace. Elizabeth welcomed Mama into heaven about eighteen months after she herself took her place among the angels and saints.

Those were a very difficult four years. Our life was changed dramatically by the stretching of our family, but I am so glad we took Mama and Elizabeth in. I can't imagine doing otherwise. I thank God for the people who were there for me to lean on. I simply couldn't have done it without them.

Ray was as much of a caregiver for my mother and sister as I was, and a caregiver to me as well when I felt like I was going to lose it. My youngest sister and her husband moved to the area with their two sons to help us care for Mama and Liz. The boys were still young, and Mama enjoyed getting to know her grandsons while she was able to do so. My other sister, who lived in another part of the state, left her wheelchair-bound husband in the care of their grown children to come and stay with Mama and Elizabeth so that Ray and I could go away for some quality time, just the two of us. We engaged the services of a home nurse who was there anytime we needed her. She became part of our family. And there were friends, neighbors, relatives, colleagues, and professionals who made sure that I was doing okay, that I had what I needed, that I had some balance in my life.

And in their own ways, Mama and Elizabeth were part of my personal network of care. In their own ways they tended my soul and spirit. Whether it was through a smile, a hug, a game of cards, a word of thanks, a song, or a prayer, they let me know in countless ways that I was needed, appreciated, and deeply loved. I know that Mama's song to Elizabeth was her song to me as well. It continues to echo in my memory:

You are my sunshine, my only sunshine.
You make me happy when skies are gray.

You'll never know dear, how much I love you.
Please don't take my sunshine away.

For Eileen, a cardiac care nurse, her network of care enabled her to care for her aging mother who suffered from Alzheimer's disease, and her younger sister, born with Down's Syndrome. She readily admits it was the most difficult thing she has ever done in her life, as well as the most rewarding.

I GET BY WITH A LITTLE HELP FROM MY FRIENDS.

John Lennon and Paul McCartney

7

Find Comfort in Routine

AFTER THE ECSTASY, THE LAUNDRY.

Jack Kornfield

Our schnauzer knows the routine. We finish dinner and clean up. Kele sticks close by me after that, following every move. I brush my teeth while she waits at the door. She sits in front of me as I put on my shoes or boots. Then it's to the coat closet if the season dictates such a garment. By this time, she starts her dance. It's first and goal on the one-yard line. The command to "Go get your leash" launches her into an enthusiastic romp in anticipation of her favorite activity of the day—our walk. We go through this same routine almost every day. Only dreadfully inclement weather stops us. We walk for about an hour, varying our route. Sometimes we stick to main streets; sometimes we walk through the cemetery; sometime we explore new avenues.

I love the discipline of the routine that our dog calls me to. No matter what is going on in my life, Kele needs her walk, and she knows that I need mine, too. When I plead that I'm too busy, she gives me a look that says, "I'll wait until later. But we're going." When I insist that it's raining too hard, her face says, "No dog or human ever melted in the rain. Get your coat on." When I complain that I'm tired because I just shoveled the entire driveway after a morning snowfall, her eyes light up as if to say, "I'll bet the cemetery looks gorgeous right now. Let's go check it out." Our daily walks give me a chance to breathe deeply, clear my mind, think about what's going on, plan, dream, pray, and remember.

When life is nothing but routine it becomes mechanical and tedious. One can go through a life of routine without ever really thinking about it, enduring a kind of intellectual atrophy where active thought is replaced by reflex motion. The American novelist Gertrude Atherton wrote, "The final result of too much routine is death in life."

However, when we find ourselves in tough situations that turn our lives upside down for a while, it is somehow comforting to be able to answer honestly, "Nothing!" when someone asks, "What's new?" Routine can be a way of grounding ourselves during an otherwise tumultuous time. It is a time when putting one foot in front of the other is done on level ground, and not the uphill climb that adversity offers.

Routine is not the same as *normalcy,* though it can be. Normal is a concept that is so individualized that it has no real meaning for human beings as a species. Normalcy is not defined by any one person or culture, even though we would like to think that we personally define it and often act and speak as if it is so. As the saying goes, "Normal is just a setting on your dryer." Your normal day and my normal day are likely to include very different activities and schedules. But our routines contribute to what we consider to be normalcy *for us.* When we are in the midst of challenging times, we welcome the routines that make life normal for us and treasure the "normal days" that come our way. They are gifts that enable us to compose ourselves and regroup.

Mary Jean Irion, a writer, poet, and teacher, captures the gift of such a day in *Yes, World,* a book of essays:

> Normal day, let me be aware of the treasure you are. Let me learn from you, love you, savor you, bless you before you depart. Let me not pass you by in quest of some rare and perfect tomorrow. Let me hold you while I may, for it will not always be so. One day I shall dig my nails into the earth, or bury my face in the pillow, or stretch myself taut, or raise my hands to the sky, and want, more than all the world, your return.

Routine and monotony are also not the same, though they can be. One person's monotony is another person's respite from the storms of life. For example, every musician, no matter the instrument, learns to do scales, arpeggios, and other technical exercises early on in his or her training. As a piano teacher, I have methodically guided countless students through such exercises and listened to millions of repetitions. There is no getting around the fact that they are boring, tedious, and yes, monotonous, but the only way to learn them is by focused repetition. Some of the more advanced students eventually recognize the value of such exercises and the implications for their musical development. As a teacher, I say a quiet prayer of thanks when that moment arrives.

My own continued pianistic development requires that I, too, play such exercises regularly. They are no more interesting to me than they are to my students, but I've come to value the time I spend on technical exercises as a respite from the bumper-car way of life that is often part of my reality. I don't have to think about them much anymore. They are routine and automatic. My fingers glide up and down the keys with ease. The muscles in my hands and arms loosen up. My breathing deepens. My mind settles into a peaceful stillness. My spirit is somehow fed through this routine that has almost become a ritual in my life.

The gift of routine is that it allows us to step back from the "high alert" status that adversity requires of us. It allows us to pay attention to people, things, and activities that build us up and make us whole. And it invites us to be more present to the moment in many ways, rendering us more approachable to those who rely on us for care.

A friend had the following conversation with her four-year-old daughter on a somewhat rare routine day that included some down time to just be together as a family:

Lucy: Guess what, Mom.

Mom: What is it, Lucy?

Lucy: When we're not doing anything, we're doing love.

To Lucy, the gift of routine was manifest as an opportunity to bask in the love of her family, reasonably assured that in the frenetic pace of life, the crises, the challenges, and the changes would be under control. For her parents, the gift of routine gave them a chance to recognize a much bigger gift: the gift of their very wise child. Finding comfort in routine during times of adversity means recognizing the opportunities to just *be* and taking advantage of them. It means being aware of the fidelity and constancy that life demands of us. And it means being thankful that life goes on.

IT'S NOT EASY TAKING MY PROBLEMS ONE AT A TIME WHEN THEY REFUSE TO GET IN LINE.

Ashleigh Brilliant

Find Comfort In Routine

- Taking inspiration from the quote by Mary Jean Irion (page 93), write your own "Ode to a Normal Day" as a tribute to the stuff of everyday life that you take for granted, but that gives shape and calmness to your life.

- Make a list of the routine activities that you enjoy doing, that you take comfort in doing, or that give you satisfaction when they're finally finished. Find some time to add pleasing activities to your day whenever possible. Be aware of the gift that they are to you in times of struggle.

- Establishing a new routine can be difficult but rewarding. Do you want to modify your present routine in any way? For example, you may want to start getting up earlier or watching less television in the evening. Is there an activity that you want to add to your life that would add some balance? It might be something like a regular exercise schedule, prayer time, reading, journal-writing, or connecting with old friends on a regular basis. Make a commitment to yourself to do this activity. Also, tell someone you trust about your commitment and ask that person to hold you to your promise.

• Make a chart of a "routine day" in your life. What happens? At what time? What is the purpose of each activity? What are positive aspects of the activities? Post your chart in a place that is readily visible so that you will be reminded to appreciate the gift of your routine every time you see it.

THE INCREDIBLE GIFT OF THE ORDINARY!
GLORY COMES STREAMING FROM THE TABLE OF DAILY LIFE.

Macrina Wiederkehr

The Maytag Man

I have a confession to make. I love doing laundry. I love the smell of clean clothes and the feel of warm clothes, fresh from the dryer. And if it's summer, all the better. I schedule my laundry days according to the weather forecast so that I can hang the laundry outside if at all possible. Nothing known to humanity smells better than bedding or towels that were dried outdoors, in the sunlight, on a breezy day. When we get to heaven I think that every day for the rest of eternity we will be given freshly laundered, sun-dried sheets and towels.

My colleagues don't know what to make of my obsession with laundry. I'm a Catholic priest, and among the many things clergy people do, laundry is not generally high on the list. They call me "the Maytag Man" and laugh that I could probably be making a heck of a lot more money if I opened my own laundry business. I have someone who comes in once a week and cleans the rectory. She would do laundry if I asked her to, but I prefer to do it myself if possible.

Traditionally in most Catholic parishes, groups like the Altar and Rosary Society or the Ladies Guild rotate responsibility for laundering altar coverings and cloths used during the liturgy. When I move to a new parish, I ask if I can help out with these things and take a place in the rotation. The women (and they are usually women who do these tasks) are startled, but willing to comply. After all, why should they have all the fun!

Why do I like doing laundry? Because every day I deal with situations that have no easy or quick resolutions. I lead a congregation in prayer, never really knowing if they are being spiritually enriched by what I say or do. I try to educate people, listen to them, nurture their gifts, pray with them, and challenge them to grow, but there are so many people in my parish that I'm not really sure I'm making an impact. I sow a lot of seeds that may or may not take root. I work with a staff that is committed to the same mission, and we share our triumphs and frustrations with each other, but results take a long time.

That's why I like doing laundry. Instant results. A purpose and a payoff. I start out with a basket of dirty clothes and linens, and a couple of hours later they are clean, fresh, and new. I know that what I did that day made an impact. Now, I know in my heart that my efforts in ministry make an impact in the long run, but doing laundry gives me a feeling of satisfaction and instant gratification.

It wasn't always this way. I'm in my sixties, and I've been a priest for more than thirty-five years. I'm ashamed to say that I used to think I was above doing laundry. One incident from my first assignment as a priest still haunts me. I was twenty-seven years old. I lived in a rectory with two other priests and a housekeeper who cooked, cleaned, did laundry, and generally took care of us. Anna was an older woman whose arthritic joints kept her in constant pain. She had a hard time moving around the rectory, especially up and down stairs, but she made do.

After lunch one day I was heading upstairs to my room. It was cold and damp outside, and Anna's arthritis was acting up. She pointed to a basket in the corner of the kitchen with my freshly laundered clothes and asked me to take it upstairs. I was in a hurry and I snapped back at her, "I did *not* become a priest to take care of laundry!" and I went upstairs, leaving the basket behind. When I got back to my room later that day, my clothes were in my drawers and my bedding was fresh. I didn't think much about it. I figured that was her job; it's what she got paid to do. Anna never said anything about the incident nor did she ever ask me to take my laundry upstairs again.

I've learned a lot about arrogance, compassion, and respect since that shameful day. And maybe my passion for the routine of doing laundry has something to do with atoning for my sin of pride. Whatever the reasons, I take great comfort in knowing that something I do that day will make a positive difference, and maybe even ease another person's burden just a little.

This story comes from Father Jim, a Catholic priest in the midwest, who is looking forward to retirement. He insists, however, that he will keep doing his own laundry as long as he is able.

IN THE RIGHT LIGHT, AT THE RIGHT
TIME, EVERYTHING IS EXTRAORDINARY.

Aaron Rose

Remember the Bells

"You forgot the milk, Mom!" my exasperated fourteen-year-old son cried out. I had gone to the grocery store after work to pick up a few things; with a fourteen-year-old boy in the house, who was in the middle of his growth spurt, we were frequently out of the staples. But I forgot the milk.

This night, as most nights, Peter was getting ready to have his bowl of Cheerios. Dinner had quickly metabolized in his growing body, which cried out for more food. Cheerios had been one of Peter's favorites as a toddler, and I usually gave him a bowl before bedtime. Now in his teens, he renewed the ritual on his own. He even remarked one thoughtful evening, "Remember when you used to give me this stuff when I was a kid? It's a good taste—in my mouth and in my mind."

But this evening Peter was angry that I forgot the milk. He was angry that I got home late from work. He was angry about a lot of other things as well. The woman who stays with Peter and his younger sister until I get home left as soon as I walked in the door. She'd had it with him.

Peter had a frustrating day at school, not an unusual occurrence. Though kind, loving, and caring, he often got angry and lashed out at schoolmates and teachers to the point of alienating them all. When Peter left middle school, he had no real friends, a reputation as a troublemaker, and a dismal academic record. We've been seeing a counselor for about a year. Now, in these first months of high school, I could tell Peter was trying really hard to do better.

After I got settled in, I tried to make up for forgetting the milk by making Peter a batch of French toast. It worked. He calmed down and ate what was probably his sixth meal of the day. Sensing that he was open to conversation I said, "Sounds like you've had a frustrating day. What happened?" His first reply was a standard one: "Nothing." I've learned to be patient, though.

"We had an English test today. I thought I knew the stuff, but Mr. Cosgrove asked different things than I knew. It's not like I didn't read the book. I did. But I left it here this weekend when I went to Dad's, so I didn't look it over."

I could tell he was sincere and disappointed that his work would not pay off. I affirmed his effort: "Peter, I believe you. But it helps to look things over before a test. Next time we'll have to make sure you take all your books to Dad's."

Peter's next words didn't shock me, but they saddened me. "Mom, I wish everything could be the same as it was before. You, Dad, me, Molly, here in this house, doing the things we always did." Peter's dad and I divorced about three years ago. It was hardest for Peter, who was eleven at the time. Both the children spend at least part of each weekend with their Dad and some days during the week if I have to go out of town.

"What do you wish was the same, Peter?" I asked.

"Well, you know how when we were little, every Saturday morning we would climb into bed with you and Dad and watch cartoons? Now when Saturday comes, I usually have to get up, pack my stuff, and head out to Dad's. I'd just like to sleep in and take it easy on Saturday morning." I could tell that my thoughtful son was just beginning to list his grievances, so I kept quiet. "Besides that, it always seems like whatever I need while I'm gone is at the other parent's house. Like that book. It's frustrating, Mom."

I assured Peter that I understood, and that we would talk with his Dad about a better arrangement. He was not finished, though. "Since you and Dad broke up and you got that new job, I'm never quite sure what the routine is around here. And that's frustrating too. I like to know these things."

I remembered back to Peter's early school days when he first learned about calendars. He had a big one in his room that he insisted we keep up-to-date. Every weekend we went through a little ritual when we wrote "school" on every school day, "soccer" on practice or game days, and made note of birthday parties, holidays, and family events. I reminded him of that practice. "Yeah, I guess I was the same way when I was a kid, huh? Things don't change much." We chuckled.

Peter's next memory startled me a bit. "Remember the bells, Mom?"

"What bells?" I asked, not having a clue what my son was talking about.

"The church bells! After dinner, we'd all go for a walk

or a bike ride, and we'd always hear the bells. You would make us stop and listen."

Then I remembered vividly. Every evening, three churches grace the town with a hymn on their respective carillons: All Saints after the six o'clock chimes; Saint Michael at six-thirty; and Redeemer at seven. I *loved* those bells and I wanted my children to grow up appreciating them and understanding the importance of taking time in the day to listen to them. I had forgotten, but my son had not. It was part of the routine—the rituals of his life—that he remembered fondly and missed.

"Peter, I forgot about those bells! Let's make a promise to each other that every time we're here we'll listen to the bells, take a deep breath, and remember all the good things about the day—just like we used to. I'll try to be home in time so that you, Molly, and I can listen together."

My son—my lanky, hungry, growing, thoughtful, sentimental son—got up from the table and turned to go to his room. As he started up the stairs he looked at me and said, "See you in the yard tomorrow at six o-clock sharp!" He took another step and looked back at me, "And *please* bring home some milk! I need my Cheerios."

This story comes from a friend who is divorced and has two children—a fourteen-year old son and a ten-year-old daughter—both of whom are bright, articulate, and fun to be with. Her son, in particular, struggles with the divorce and the new lifestyle it has meant for all of them.

RITUALS ARE FORMULAS BY WHICH HARMONY IS RESTORED.

Terry Tempest Williams

8

Be Open to the Hidden Gifts

SOME LUCK LIES IN NOT GETTING WHAT
YOU THOUGHT YOU WANTED BUT
GETTING WHAT YOU HAVE, WHICH ONCE
YOU HAVE GOT IT YOU MAY BE SMART
ENOUGH TO SEE IS WHAT YOU WOULD
HAVE WANTED HAD YOU KNOWN.

Garrison Keillor

There is a story of an old Chinese farmer who owned an old horse that he used for tilling his fields. One day the horse escaped into the hills. When all the farmer's neighbors sympathized with the old man over his bad luck, the farmer replied, "Bad luck? Good luck? Who knows?" A week later the horse returned with a herd of wild horses from the hills and this time the neighbors congratulated the farmer on his good luck. His reply was "Good luck? Bad luck? Who knows?" Then, when the farmer's son was attempting to tame one of the wild horses, he fell off its back and broke his leg. Everyone thought this was very bad luck. Not the farmer, whose only reaction was "Bad luck? Good luck? Who knows?" Some weeks later the army marched into the village and conscripted every able-bodied youth they found there. When they saw the farmer's son with his broken leg they let him off. Was that good luck? Bad luck? Who knows?

The farmer, with wisdom borne of a lifetime of experience, knew that the obvious conclusion might not be the correct one. In his consistent reply to his neighbors, he admonished them to wait and see what happened next, remaining open to the idea that what had happened next may have been a blessing or a curse, and that the observable circumstances had little to do with it. This is a hard lesson for most of us to learn.

It is often difficult to see the gifts in a tough situation, because we are so focused on just making it through. When things are going well none of us want to think about negative outcomes. Sometimes it takes a little time and effort on our part to finally see and embrace the gifts that come from tough times. Many factors contribute to our failure to recognize these gifts, but three factors in particular warrant soul-searching:

Be open. We have to be willing to put aside our haughtiness and let go of notions of the way things *should* be. For example, I live in a county that has one of the highest rates of teen pregnancy in the nation. There are likely a lot of reasons for this dubious distinction, but the fact is that it is our reality.

My extended family includes many young moms who contributed to that statistic. Announcement of their pregnancies turned life upside down for their parents and grandparents, most of whom were shocked, hurt, disappointed, and experienced all the other emotions that accompany such unplanned and unexpected events. Chastisement was met with icy stares and protests. Advice to place these babies for adoption was ignored. Eventually things quieted down, relatives rallied, the babies were born, and they are growing up in the care of extended families, surrounded by loads of love. These children bring great joy to all of us. They are gifts borne of adversity and hope for the future.

Be fearless. Another reason it may be difficult to see the gifts hidden by adversity is fear. Many people live by the adage, "A bird in the hand is worth two in the bush." We value the known, and we fear the unknown. No matter how burdensome life may be, we are hesitant to make the changes necessary to get to a better place. We fear that the result of the change or the process of change itself will be more difficult than the day-to-day existences we currently endure. We may even fear success. After all, when we are in the midst of trying times, success is something elusive and therefore, unfamiliar.

The following story serves as an example of failing to recognize gifts out of fear.

Jim worked for an engineering firm for twelve years. He was miserable. He hung on to the job even though he was unhappy, wanting to make it work for his family. He drew a good salary, the kids were settled, and his wife liked her job. But after one particularly tense meeting, Jim confronted his manager and the vice president of the department. The result was a forced resignation.

Jim deeply regretted his actions and considered going back to his supervisor to apologize. His wife, who knew how unhappy he was, talked him out of it. He went to an employment agency and saw the following sign in the counselor's office: "'Getting fired is nature's way of telling you that you had the wrong job in the first place.'—Hal Lancaster in *The Wall Street Journal*." Jim hoped with all his heart that was true.

Eventually he found another job. It meant a move for his family, a new job for his wife, and new schools and new friends for their children. That was six years ago. Everyone is happily settled again, and Jim whistles as he walks to work every day.

Now Jim recognizes the gift that came out of that tough time in his life; it was a gift that was hidden by his fear of making a change.

Be forgiving. Finally, sometimes we cannot recognize gifts that rise from adversity because we are reluctant to forgive. Anger, pain, grudges, shame, resentment—all things that stand in the way of seeing hidden gifts—may be directed at another person, an institution, or at oneself. These emotions form an impassible curtain that completely covers the window of the soul, allowing no light to penetrate and making it difficult to see the gifts hidden in the darkness of the heart. We see and hear about the failure to forgive all the time:

- The parents who are angry about their child's choice of a spouse and refuse to attend the wedding or have any future contact, cutting themselves off from their new grandchild;

- The man who decides that he will no longer attend church because he disagrees with its leadership, eliminating the possibility that he can impact change in the system and removing himself from a supportive community;

- The woman who makes an error in judgment that results in significant embarrassment for her employer and quits her job out of guilt and shame, even though her employer is willing to let her make a fresh start because she is good at what she does, and he knows it will not happen again.

Someone once said, "Forgiveness is letting go of the hope for a better past." When we let go of that regret, we are free to hope for a better future. The future may be filled with tough times—because life is like that—but it will also be filled with hidden gifts just waiting to be discovered.

YOU ARE IN YOUR OWN WAY. PLEASE STAND ASIDE.

from a fortune cookie

Be Open to the Hidden Gifts

- Find a small box with a lid and wrap each piece in pretty paper so that you can remove the top without unwrapping the box. Put the box in a place where it will be in your view as you move about your day. When you recognize a gift that comes from adversity, write a description of the gift and how you came to recognize it on a small card or piece of paper. Then put it in the box. Every month or so review the contents of your box. Say a prayer of gratitude.

- If asked to do so, what story from your life would you add to this chapter of the book? Write a story about a time in your life when you recognized a gift peeking or elbowing through adversity.

- Consider the following questions:

    - In what situations do your prejudices or attitudes stop you from seeing the hidden gifts? What keeps you from being open to possibilities? What will you do about it?

    - What are you afraid of? That is, what keeps you from making changes that you know you need to make? What gifts might await you if you let go of your fears?

    - Are there difficult memories that constantly come to the front of your mind? What might happen if you let go of your "hope for a better past"? What steps will you take to make this happen?

- At the end of every day, answer this question: "What am I grateful for today?" You may want to write your answers in your journal or on a sheet of paper that you can post in a visible place. Or, at night before you go to sleep, tell a loved one about each gift from the day for which you are grateful; invite her or him to do likewise.

Everything happening, great and small, is a parable whereby God speaks to us, and the art of life is to get the message.

Malcolm Muggeridge

Barren and Blessed

Almost every woman alive grows up assuming that she will one day bring new life into the world. When we reach puberty, our bodies go through the biological changes necessary to make that happen. However, long before we reach adolescence we are convinced that motherhood is a part of our destiny, a reason for being.

And so it was for me. I grew up in a large extended family where no one was single or childless by the time they reached age thirty. One after the other my cousins and younger siblings married, became pregnant, and took their rightful place in the "circle of life." Some were very young when they married, barely out of their teens. Others were in their late twenties. But they got married. They had children. And that was what life was supposed to be like.

I decided to go to college and then to graduate school, providing a convenient deferment from traditional expectations. My parents hoped that I would meet the man of my dreams in grad school and eventually do what it was I was supposed to be doing with my life. I expected the same, though I was averse to the spouse safari that some of my peers seemed to be on. I figured I had plenty of time to find a mate, and I was convinced that children would come after that. I had no reason to think otherwise. I was a young, healthy, fertile woman.

In my thirtieth year, something happened to my menstrual cycle. Prior to that time I could pretty much set a clock by the regularity of my cycle. But that year I would start and stop and start again. I missed my target date by weeks or was two weeks early. I was in the midst of making the switch from life as an academic to life as a youth minister, and I presumed that the stress was taking its toll on my body. In early December of that year I started my period; it didn't stop again for twenty-five months.

My doctor ordered tests. They all came back negative. He prescribed four different medications in those two years, two of which had no effect and two that made me want to climb the walls. Two minor surgical procedures stopped the flow for about ten days each time. As a last resort he ordered an experimental drug designed to affect hormone production and cause the blood to stop flowing. It had the opposite effect. The doctor finally admitted that he had no idea what the problem was, or why the treatments didn't work. We had no other options left, he said. I needed to have a hysterectomy. I was thirty-two years old. I gladly agreed, wanting more than anything to end the problem. I was exhausted, anemic, and scared.

During my final appointment before the surgery, the doctor offered all kinds of information, as he was required to do. I had to sign a paper indicating that I understood the physical ramifications of the surgery: permanent sterility. Yes, I knew all that. I just wanted to get it over with; to get on with my life. The surgery went fine, the problem ended, and I gained back my strength.

However, I was not prepared for the emotional wounds that remained long after the physical wounds had healed. At no point did my doctor bring up the psychological ramifications, the emotional trauma, or the spiritual barrenness that would result from such a drastic change. The day I came home from the hospital was the day my youngest sister had her first child. I sobbed on and off all day. Yes, some of those tears were tears of joy for Cindy and Gary, who had waited a long time to conceive. But the tears were mostly for my own loss and the deep pain of knowing that I would never experience the same joy of bringing a child into this world.

For a few years I struggled with this new void in my body and in my life. When I tried to shop for toys or children's clothing at Christmas time, It was all I could do not to burst into tears in the middle of the store. I avoided walking through children's departments. I avoided looking at new babies and shunned extended contact with young children. I struggled to play piano through a first Eucharist liturgy at my church and had to work hard to focus on the music and not on the angelic faces that were being celebrated that day.

Time, the great healer, eventually helped me accept the fact that I would not give birth to children. Along with the acceptance came a new appreciation for the miracle of life and the gift of children. I always liked children, but now I delight in them. I love talking with them, playing with them, and teaching them. I recognize their wisdom, value their ideas, respect them, and lobby for their causes. I love them at all ages and stages, right through the tumultuous years of adolescence. I remember hearing a speaker once say that children and teenagers need someone who is head-over-heels in love with them besides their parents. I figured out that I could be that person, if only for a short time in a child's life.

Being childless allows me to be present to children and teenagers in ways a parent cannot be. I know that I have a gift to offer them. But the gift they offer me is far greater. I no longer have the ability to birth new life, but children provide me with daily opportunities to nurture life.

TO GAIN THAT WHICH IS WORTH
HAVING, IT MAY BE NECESSARY TO LOSE
EVERYTHING ELSE.

Josephine Bernadette Devlin

The Anklebone's Connected to the . . . Head?

I didn't know why, but my ankle hurt badly. I went to an orthopedic physician who specialized in such conditions. The orthopedist did what he could, but nothing seemed to work. Apparently, the ligament kept popping up or out or in or whatever it is ligaments do. He couldn't fix it, nor could he find the reason it was acting that way. Finally, he suggested that I see a neurologist. I protested that the problem was in my ankle, not in my head, but I made an appointment. There were X-rays, CT scans, MRIs, and a battery of other tests as the neurologist searched for the cause of my problem.

My family and I were shocked by the diagnosis: brain cancer. How could this be? I was thirty-four years old with three young children. What would my family do if something happened to me? The next few weeks were a whirlwind. There were visits to doctors, all kinds of tests, a hospital stay, and a prolonged and delicate surgery. I recovered slowly. I expected to have to spend time in a rehab facility, but the doctors sent me home instead. I got the impression that doctors just don't think you're going to make if you have certain kinds of brain tumors, so they didn't think that rehab was going to be necessary. They gave me about two years to live. That was more than ten years ago.

Brain cancer took a lot of things away from me, both mentally and physically. I can't do the things I used to do. I used to be active and always on the go; now I'm slow. I can't even ride a bike by myself. My husband finally went out and bought a tandem bike so we could ride together. Sometimes I feel like a burden on my family. They've all been supportive, but I'm not used to being taken care of. I'm a wife and a mom, so I'm usually the one who is doing the caring. There are times when I get depressed about it all, but then I remember that I am living a miracle.

I now think of my brain cancer as kind of a gift from God; it enabled me to recognize other gifts in my life. I am much closer to God now than I ever have been. I realize that this God who created me loves me, cares for me, and wants only the best for me. The whole time I was ill, i kept praying and asking everyone to pray for me. Whenever my husband ran into anyone we knew he would ask for prayers, whether it was in the middle of the grocery store or the children's sports practices. I think God got a little annoyed with all the prayers on my behalf and just decided to heal me so that the onslaught of requests would stop!

I have also gained many new and special friends as a result of my illness. I joined a support group for people with brain tumors. I've come to realize that I've been very blessed. Some people with brain tumors aren't nearly as lucky as I have been. They lose various physical and mental functions; their once full lives come to a screeching halt. At least mine just slowed down.

The word that sums up my feelings about the last ten years is *gratitude*. I live life now much more aware of everything. I learned to slow down the pace of my life (most of the time), and I stop to enjoy the sunrises and sunsets that I once took for granted. I am grateful every morning that I am able to wake up and thank God for another day. I am grateful for the people in my life and for all that is around me and within me. I am grateful for the gift of life itself.

Rose lives in Western New York with her husband, three children, a couple of lizards, and a cat.

HOW HAPPY A PERSON IS DEPENDS
UPON THE DEPTH OF HIS GRATITUDE.

John Miller

9

Find Hope in the Moment

THE NATURAL FLIGHTS OF THE HUMAN
MIND ARE NOT FROM PLEASURE TO
PLEASURE, BUT FROM HOPE TO HOPE.

Samuel Johnson

By nature, I tend toward pessimism. I see the glass as half empty, the clouds without the silver lining, and the rain instead of the rainbow. If there is a down side to something, I'm the one who is likely to point it out. I am apt to overlook the good and see only the bad and the ugly. I try to curb my pessimism as much as I can, though sometimes I catch myself not only holding on to unpleasant realities of the past but being prematurely disappointed in the future. I take comfort in George Will's words in *The Leveling Wind*: "The nice part about being a pessimist is that you are constantly being either proven right or pleasantly surprised."

I have a close friend who is the exact opposite; he calls himself a "pathological optimist." When things get rough he is never down for more than a short time before he begins to see the glass half full, the silver lining, and the rainbow. Someone said that, "Optimism is a cheerful frame of mind that enables a teakettle to sing though in hot water up to its nose." That's Tom. He is always ready to put a positive spin on what may appear to me to be a disaster in the making. He is like the person who (as the story goes), when falling from the top of a skyscraper, says at every floor "I'm all right so far." He readily admits that pessimists are more in touch with reality, though he points out that optimists are probably happier.

In our work and in our friendship we balance each other nicely. I am able to identify the down side of a situation, while he is able to find the gift. I can name the grim realities; he can see the hopeful possibilities. We have learned a lot from each other, though. A gifted man in many ways, his greatest gift is perhaps his hopefulness. In his presence—whether or not we are actually in the same place at the same time—I can be an optimist, and in mine he can explore the negative side of a situation. From Tom I learned to hope in spite of a dismal forecast. From me he learned that hope does not necessarily mean that nothing will go wrong. In fact, something probably will.

Because we are human, we hope. We hope for the impossible, the improbable, the implausible, and the unlikely. We hope in spite of, in the face of, and in case of. We hope for the best, and we hope for the hopeless. We were hoped into existence by our parents and launched into the world by that same hope. We hope because it is our nature to be hopeful. It gives us a reason to get up in the morning and reassurance that allows us to sleep at night. We hope because we are made in the image and likeness of the One who created us, the God of all hope.

Being able to find hope in every moment is an important skill for someone in the midst of a struggle.

Hope enables us to move from one thing to the next, confident that each move will get us closer to the goal. When all seems lost, somehow we find it in ourselves to say, "There's always tomorrow."

There is no way to describe hope. It's something we feel as well as something we do. Every parent knows what hope feels like; every child does it. Every unemployed person knows the feeling, and every student waiting for a report card or award has the technique of hoping down to a science. Every sick person knows hope as a feeling and as an act, as does anyone who has ever struggled with a relationship, faced a financial crisis, suffered through a disaster, lobbied for a cause, nursed a sick relative, or tried to impact a broken system.

Though not the same, hope is intimately connected with faith. John Calvin wrote, "The word *hope* I take for faith; and indeed hope is nothing else but the constancy of faith." Though people of faith are not necessarily always hope-filled, they take comfort in knowing that there is a source of hope, a being in which they can place their hope, a higher power. These people have hope because of their faith, and they have faith because of their hope.

A few years ago I was playing the game *Trouble* with my four-year-old great niece. Victoria loved this game. She especially loved the plastic bubble in the middle of the game board, because when she pressed it and then let go, the dice inside the bubble rattled around and came to rest on one side. Then she got to count the number of dots on the dice and move her piece. Every time Victoria popped the bubble and moved her piece she exclaimed, "I won! I won!" with a huge smile, just because she got a number and moved a few spaces. I don't remember who if anyone won that game in the way intended by the manufacturers, but I know that Tori won every time it was her turn.

How wonderful to consider every move in life a winning one, a hopeful one! How marvelous to consider every number that comes up, every event, every moment, a winning moment! To her, the final outcome was not as important as the joy she experienced along the way. A number that caused her to go back to the beginning was as much a source of joy as one that got a peg in her home base, because it meant that she got to do it all over again. Winning the game did not matter to her as much as winning the moment.

My optimistic friend Tom is right. The happiest people in the world are probably not those who experience little adversity in their life. The happiest people are the optimistic ones, the ones who are most hopeful and hope-filled. They know what to look for when they sift through the remains of the day. They look for the shreds of hope—their winning moments—gather them up, and embrace them tightly with the arms of their soul.

THERE ARE VICTORIES OF THE SOUL AND SPIRIT.

SOMETIMES, EVEN IF YOU LOSE, YOU WIN.

Elie Wiesel

Find Hope in the Moment

- Consider the following quotes about hope. Find others or create your own "Hope is . . ." statements to add to the list. Write these quotes on a small pad of colorful sticky notes. Every morning, peel and stick a new quote to your bathroom mirror so you can reflect on it as you begin your day.

- Hope is a state of mind, not of the world. (Vaclav Havel)
- Hope is the feeling we have if the feeling we have is not permanent (Mignon McLaughlin)
- Hope is . . . music played in the resurrection ashes. (Nelly Sachs)
- Hope is faith holding out its hand in the dark. (George Iles)
- Hope is grief's best music. (Henry George Bohn)
- Hope is the struggle of the soul, breaking loose from what is perishable, and attesting her eternity. (Herman Melville)
- Hope is the parent of faith. (Cyrus Bartol)
- Hope is slowly extinguished and quickly revived. (Sophia Lee)

- Are there shreds of hope in your life right now? That is, do you see signs that all is not lost, that things will get better? Make a list of these signs in your journal and refer to it often, especially when you feel yourself slipping into the dark side of adversity. Or you might want to write each item on a small self-stick note and surround your workspace or living space with them as constant reminders.

- Are you an optimist or a pessimist? Find a book of personal style inventories—tests that help us determine various aspects of our personality—and find the inventories that deal with this topic. They may provide insight into the depth of your preference or the balance.

- Find someone you trust who is of the opposite personality type from you. If you are a pessimist, look for an optimist or vice versa. Talk with that person about a situation in your life that causes you anxiety. Explore insights, perspectives, and concrete signs of hope.

- Start each day completing the following sentence starter: "Today I hope that. . . ." At the end of the day, name something that caused you to be hopeful that day. Create a running list in your journal. At the end of every month, reread the entries for that month to reinforce the fact that you have reason to hope and are, in fact, a hopeful person.

Hope is the thing with feathers

That perches in the soul

And sings the tune without the words

And never stops at all.

Emily Dickinson

My Brother the Thief

I am so embarrassed about this I'm not sure I even want to tell you. No one outside my family knows. At least I don't think they do. Not even my best friend. And we tell each other everything. I'm just not ready to tell her yet. You know my brother, David? He may be going to jail for three to fifteen years. Investment fraud. That's a nice way of saying my brother is a thief. God only knows how many people he's swindled money from. The prosecuting attorneys are in the process of interviewing his clients.

Do you know how I found out? My cousin saw it in the newspaper a couple of months ago. She called me recently and asked how David was doing. I must have sounded confused because she told me about the charges. She also told me that according to the article he was charged and convicted of the same crime six years ago. He never fulfilled the terms of his sentence, so he has little hope of avoiding jail this time around, especially since the same judge is on the case. We never knew about that incident either.

My poor mother is so upset, she cries every time she talks about it. He bilked her out of about two hundred thousand dollars. He lost it all. Now when she should be enjoying her retirement with no worries, she has to watch every penny. When I get angry, she says, "David is sick. He wouldn't be doing this if he wasn't sick." He's sick all right. Sick with envy. Sick with greed. He lives around people with money, and he wants to be just like them. He wants the best of everything. His house is gorgeous. He's got expensive cars. His kids go to private colleges and he foots the bill. On the outside it looks like he's got a life just like his neighbors'. In a way, I hope that he really is mentally ill. It would help us all to know that he didn't purposefully hurt his mother.

It's like he's got two personalities. One David is a wonderful father, a devout person, and a pillar of his church. The other David is a liar and a thief. He's shifty and never answers a question directly. You could ask him, "What color is the sky today, David?" and his answer would be something like, "It's a beautiful day, isn't it?" We should have seen this coming.

He's always been hard to get close to, even when we were young. He never went in the same direction the rest of us did. My siblings and I went to college. David went into the Navy at seventeen.

My sister Debbie won't talk about all of this. Besides, her mother-in-law just died, and her husband is showing signs that his cancer has returned. She doesn't need the added aggravation of David's antics. My brother Dennis, well, he's such a good guy. He just can't understand how David could do anything like this, especially to his own mother.

Like I said, I'm embarrassed. You know why I'm embarrassed? Because I'm a teacher. Every day I talk to kids about making good choices. We sing songs about making good choices and talk about how bad choices have consequences. It's my mantra. And here's my own brother, making bad choice after bad choice. I'm embarrassed because I had no clue. He duped us all. He lied to us, and we fell for it. Even his stationery used false names to make it sound like he was part of a big firm. I'm embarrassed because I had no clue that he was doing this kind of stuff for the last twenty years.

I'm angry for what he is doing to Mom. She's worried sick. The woman has a very bad heart to begin with; if anything happens to her. . . . It's hard to watch something like this happen in the family. I want to make things right for mom, but I feel pretty helpless and confused right now. There's nothing I can do except listen to my mother cry, and when she wonders where she went wrong all I can tell her is that it's not her fault. It's so very sad.

I keep looking for signs of hope, but it's very hard to see them right now. David is seeing a psychotherapist. He finally realizes that he needs help. I'm hopeful that counseling will help him and that he will understand that he doesn't have to impress everyone. Maybe David and his family will take a look at what they have and understand that keeping up with the Joneses is not necessary to live a happy life.

I'm hopeful that as a man in his mid-forties he can start to live an honest life and work an honest job. At his core David is a good person who did something bad, and good people can't stay bad forever. And my mother—I think she understands that this is not her fault. At least I hope she does.

Right now, about all we can do is hope. Our family is strong. We *will* get through this, just like we've gotten through all the other crises in our lives. And that fact gives me the most hope of all.

This story is from someone who did not want to be identified. The situation is still unfolding and preserving the family's anonymity is important.

THE LONGEST DAY MUST HAVE ITS CLOSE—THE GLOOMIEST NIGHT WILL WEAR ON TO A MORNING.

Harriet Beecher Stowe

From Darkness to Hope

Many years ago, Dan and I were enveloped in personal, private sadness. We had lost our unborn child at just nine week's gestation. I know women miscarry all the time, but this child was a gift conceived after three years of expensive and painful fertility treatments. I was filled with sorrow.

We went about our daily lives because we had to, but my smile was simply camouflage. We continued to try to conceive. Some of our friends and family joked about "how fun" it must be trying. They were so wrong. That beautiful union of bodies between married people becomes clinical and stressful when fertility issues are in the middle of it all.

I prayed constantly, my way, chatting with God. No poetry or repetition. Not like the prayers of my mother or grandmother. One day I received a booklet from my mom containing prayers for a nine-day novena. My mom was big on novenas. Catholic women of her generation put great faith in saying specific prayers for each of the nine days. Some novenas were made to Mary or various saints, and others to the Sacred Heart of Jesus. Though it was not my style of prayer, I felt so empty and wanted a child so badly, that I decided to try praying the novena. Why not?

In the first few days of the novena I said the required prayer. That was that. On with life. But one day was different. I prayed the prayer for that day. It read, "Your soul a sword shall pierce so that many hearts may be revealed." In that moment, with that prayer, I felt an incredible hope fill my soul. I felt truly filled with God's presence. I realized that my soul had already been pierced, and the hearts to be revealed to me would come through adoption. In a minute or so that stunning powerful feeling waned, but I was left with this revelation and this hope.

My husband and I had talked about adopting a child, knowing that parenting wasn't about biology, but about love. We had not given up the quest of conceiving again, but that day the curtains of sadness lifted, and I knew that my destiny as a mother wasn't in the hands of the doctor anymore. God showed me the path, and my husband and I followed it into hope and joy.

We now have two beautiful sons, born of other women. Through these women, God gave our boys life; my husband and I help them to live it. After going through the adoption process twice, we remained so interested in the issues that we were trained as pre-adoption counselors for people interested in starting their own families through adoption. Some of their stories are painful, like ours. Others are joyful. But no matter the reason these couples are considering adoption, they are all filled with hope.

Mary Ellen and Dan live in Oregon with their two sons, Jordan and Aidan. Their primary work is delighting in and caring for their family.

FAITH IS THE CENTERPIECE OF A CONNECTED LIFE. IT ALLOWS US TO LIVE BY THE GRACE OF INVISIBLE STRANDS.

Terry Tempest Williams

1 0

Celebrate the Light

NEVER FEAR SHADOWS. THEY SIMPLY
MEAN THERE'S A LIGHT SHINING
SOMEWHERE NEARBY.

Ruth E. Renkel

I was driving and listening to a variety-type radio show on an empty stretch of the New York State Thruway early one Saturday morning when I heard a story that made me laugh out loud:

> One day Jim took his three-year-old son, Josh, out to do some errands. His wife, Karen, had recently given birth to a new baby, and she needed to rest while the baby was sleeping. They were thinking of doing some remodeling in their home, so one of the stops that day was a building supply store that had a huge area of kitchens and bathrooms on display. The father and son walked around amidst the models, Josh opening cupboards and drawers and generally amusing himself, as three-year-olds are wont to do.

After a while Jim lost sight of his son and didn't hear him moving around the models. He had a moment of panic and started yelling the boy's name. "Josh, where are you? Joshua?" Then he heard a familiar voice. "I'm here, Dad."

Jim followed the sound of his son's voice and finally found him sitting on a display toilet . . . with his pants down around his ankles! Jim's worst fear was confirmed when Josh looked up at him with a beaming face and said, "Wipe me, Daddy."

Jim looked around, totally embarrassed by what had just transpired. He was thankful no one was around at the moment. He did not want to admonish the boy, because it was the first time Joshua had taken the initiative and sat on a toilet to move his bowels. Jim knew it was a moment to be celebrated. He could not find toilet paper and had no tissue, so he pulled up Josh's pants, put the cover down on the toilet, and they hurried out of the store. He knew that a sales person or maintenance worker would get a rude awakening some time that day, but he was too embarrassed to tell anyone.

When they got home, Josh ran into the house yelling "Mommy! I went on the toilet all by myself and made a BM!" Karen enthusiastically congratulated her very proud little boy, but she knew there was more to the story by the look on Jim's face. It could wait though; they had something to celebrate right now. And celebrate they did—with a round of ice cream cones.

The story of Josh's triumph illustrates an important point about living through tough times: even when we're dealing with an adverse situation and things look pretty bleak, there is always a light shining through. That light needs to be recognized, held on to, and celebrated.

For all that goes wrong in our life, somewhere there is a light shining through. Sometimes the light is obvious. We can appreciate the first downs we accumulate on the gridiron of our lives, because we know that if we get enough first downs we eventually score. We're even willing to put up with a few sacks, endure a bad call now and then, and forgive people for their fumbles or dropped passes—as long as the first downs keep coming.

At other times, though, it takes some effort on our part to recognize the light, and even more effort to hold on to it when things get really rough. Though in our heads we believe that the light will eventually break through, our hearts often get lost in what the poet John Milton calls "darkness visible." We focus on the struggle, the loss, and the pain. And though those things are undeniable and need our attention, surviving tough times requires that we recognize when survival is indeed a possibility and believe that the light will eventually prevail.

The following examples are from people who recognized the light and held on to it, believing that the light would eventually lead them to a place of joy:

- Alice's mother was fading. She lost most of her sight and hearing and was also losing her sense of touch. Daily she wondered aloud about how she came to be so decrepit. She could not understand why God neither cured nor retrieved her body. Because her mother's demise was slow, Alice and her sisters had an opportunity to gradually say good-bye. That was Alice's "light." She knew that their grief would not be lessened when her mother finally died, but she also knew that it would be easier to let their mother go having had so much time with her.

- Mark's wife lost her job as principal of a private school. Their family's income was cut in half, even though their expenses remained the same, with a daughter in college and another in high school. They adjusted their spending habits, and Carol took part-time jobs, one of which eventually resulted in full-time employment. Mark saw his "light" in many aspects of the difficult change. Carol's stress level in her new job was significantly lower than it was as principal, and the change gave her an opportunity to explore options outside of the education field. He also knew that the family's spending adjustments would have long-term benefits.

- Anne and Jeanne became close friends through some community projects they worked on together. Each of them went through a painful period of soul-searching and came to the realization that their attraction to each other was more than friendship; it was a sexual attraction as well. They decided to move in together and build a life. They shared the news cautiously, but were deeply hurt many times in the process by people they thought were friends, people they hoped would understand and support them. Through it all, they kept their eye on their "light," saying, "We have each other, and deep inside we know it's right. The bottom line is that neither of us has ever been happier."

• Jennifer's seven-year relationship with Jason had come to an end. The last two years had been painfully rocky, and she finally came to terms with the fact that she needed to look elsewhere for the soul mate that she so desired. She had finally begun to believe in herself and in her ability to create a good life for herself and Tori, her young daughter. In all the pain of ending the relationship, Jennifer held on to the "light" that Jason, though not Tori's biological father, was every bit her "daddy" and had been so since he first came into their lives. Jennifer knew that Jason would continue to love Tori deeply, take care of her needs, and worry about her happiness.

Besides recognizing and holding onto our light, we need to acknowledge it in some way. For Karen, Jim, and Joshua it meant celebratory ice cream cones. For Anne and Jeanne, such celebrations took the form of little getaways to places they both enjoyed. For Mark it meant deep breaths and confident prayers of thanksgiving knowing that all would be well. These acknowledgments can be quiet and simple: a moment of silent recognition, an admission of triumph; or they can be elaborate and extensive: a celebratory meal, a basket of flowers.

Celebrating the light that shines through tough times ultimately means a recognition that our struggles are temporary; adversity is a detour, and tough times are just that: *times*. A moment, not a permanent state of being. It means knowing that though there are shadows, there is always light.

HAPPINESS IS DIFFERENT FROM PLEASURE. HAPPINESS HAS SOMETHING TO DO WITH STRUGGLING AND ENDURING AND ACCOMPLISHING.

George Sheehan

Celebrate the Light

- The philosopher Søren Kierkegaard wrote, "It is quite true what Philosophy says: that Life must be understood backwards. But that makes one forget the other saying: that it must be lived—forwards." Reflect on a tough time in your life and look for the small light that shone through and led to more light and still more. For example, you might say "If _____ hadn't happened, then _____ wouldn't have happened, and _____ wouldn't have happened," and so forth. You may want to do this exercise in the form of a backward time line or a chart.

- Write your thoughts about the following questions in your journal or quietly meditate on them:

  - How is your life better because of the tough times you've endured?

  - Do you think your life will improve because of a struggle you are currently experiencing? In what ways?

- How do you celebrate triumphs? Give an example.

- What story from your life would you add the to the end of this chapter of the book? Write a story of recognizing light amidst the shadows, holding on to it, and celebrating it.

- Think about the "lights" that are part of your day-to-day struggles. Ritualize the process in this way:

  - Set up a space for reflection and decorate it simply with items that have meaning to you. Include a large candle and several tea light candles.

  - Light the large candle. Decide what that candle represents. For example, it might represent a holy presence or yourself.

  - Think about a struggle you are facing right now or one that you recently endured. What were the moments of light that you experienced in that struggle? It might be a connection with a friend, a sense of accomplishment, or a decision that needed to be made. Light a tea candle from the large candle for each memory of light. Say a prayer of gratitude for the light and for the memory of it.

- Make it a practice to burn a "tough times" candle regularly. Give it a place of honor in your home and burn it as a reminder of the light that shines through adversity.

IN THIS WORLD, FULL OFTEN, OUR JOYS ARE ONLY THE TENDER SHADOWS WHICH OUR SORROWS CAST.

Henry Ward Beecher

Accidental Gifts

It was a terrifying experience. On my way to the first faculty meeting of the year, I was hit by a man in a truck going seventy miles per hour through a red light. He was heading straight for my car door, but at the last millisecond he swerved and hit the car in front of my side view mirror. At impact the car burst into flames, but because my door had been spared, I was able to open it and get out. The fact that I'm alive is a true miracle.

I have been teased by many people about my actions at the time of the crash. As you might imagine I was thrown toward the opposite side of the car, but when I finally came to rest, I did three things: first, I said a prayer of thanks for my life and the fact that I was not injured in any major way. Then I called my husband to let him know what had happened and to ask him to help me. Finally, I called 911. I operated on pure instinct. I never stopped to ponder what I would do in any particular order. My actions clearly reflect my life priorities: God, family, other things. I think it's pretty amazing how these things reveal themselves.

Other than the order in which I took action, there are a few other things about the accident that stay with me. I will never forget the look in the other driver's eyes as he hit. As we locked gazes there was sheer terror there. The other thing is that in my memory the event had no sound. Common sense says that the impact had to be associated with screaming sounds of skidding tires as he tried to stop, sounds of metal crunching into accordion pleats. But in my memory the events are silent. Perhaps that ability of the psyche to block out such disturbing memories is yet another gift from God. While I will probably always be able to conjure the vision of what happened as it unfolded, with any grace at all it will only run as a silent movie.

Most of all, though, I will remember the only witness. He was very shaken by having watched the crash in progress. He stayed with me the whole time, making sure I was safe. He was afraid the car would explode so he got me out of the car and far away from it. He spoke with the police and put his name and number on a scrap of paper in my hand as I was being placed into the ambulance. At the time I remember thinking that he was surely one of those angels one hears about or reads about in books. He was a source of great comfort at a very distressing time.

At least one positive thing has come out of the accident. Because I was home for a couple of weeks after the event, I actually got to read some of the e-mail messages that I usually put in the "when I have time" file. Sitting at home nursing my bruises and whiplash, I came across an announcement for a conference in Boston that meshed perfectly with a project I've been dreaming of accomplishing for years: starting a family advocacy program at the university. Things have moved very swiftly since. As a result of the conference input and initiatives I took, the university is opening a family advocacy program to provide medical and legal services to under-served families and those who have children with disabilities. That is something that probably would not have happened if I hadn't had the accident.

In the past few months I have reflected on the goodness of God many times and the ways in which things happen for reasons beyond our knowing. That has been the story of my life; the hand of God has been in everything, giving me opportunities not only to come back from painful places, but to move forward to places I would never have discovered otherwise.

Though the accident was terribly distressing and could have been tragic, the outcome, in its own strange way, was positive and affirming. I must admit that the effects have taken a toll on me in terms of emotional and physical energy. But though I get discouraged at times, the light shines through. Mostly I am left with a profound gratitude for being alive. I am able to continue the daily rituals that comprise family life. I am continuing my work with families, teaching students, going to church, planning for my daughter's wedding, planting pansies in the front yard, and staying in touch with people that I love. I am able to hear my children's voices, and be hugged by a husband who adores me. All these things are gifts from a gracious God. All are lights in the darkness. All are reasons to celebrate, indeed.

Susan is a clinical psychologist, a nurse practitioner, and an associate professor of nursing. She and her husband Dan live in Knoxville, Tennessee and are the parents of two adult children.

LIGHT [IS] BUT THE SHADOW OF GOD.

Sir Thomas Browne

I Did It!

"Can I stay with Grammy tonight, Mom?" It was a frequent request when my niece Jaclyn was a child. "We're gonna play Barbies!" She enjoyed the undivided attention of a doting grandmother, as well as playing with Grandma's collection of toys. Since Grandma lived across the street, her parents knew that if it didn't work out they could just walk over and retrieve their little one. "Sure, Jaclyn, you can stay. But if you decide you don't want to sleep over, Daddy or I will come get you." Reassured, Jaclyn went to retrieve the dolls and the case of Barbie paraphernalia. As she did so, she waved to her mom. "Bye. I love you."

Every time Jaclyn tried to stay with Grammy, all was well until bedtime. She got into her pajamas and went to bed with her grandma at her side. They chatted, they sang, they told stories. But inevitably, the refrain, "I miss my mom and dad!" began, meaning that her overnight plans would likely be altered. Eventually she started to cry, and by about eleven o'clock she begged to go home. Grammy called her house and her mom or dad would walk across the street and get her.

It happened several times, and we knew that Jaclyn was disappointed with herself. She wanted more than anything to overcome her fear and gain a little bit of independence in the process. She tried, over and over again.

Jaclyn made plans to stay with Grammy one day when she was almost six. She and her grandmother played with her dolls all evening, as usual. She got ready for bed as usual. She laid down with Grammy at her side, as usual, and they sang and chatted and told stories, as usual. She started her "I miss my mom and dad" refrain, but then something happened. Jaclyn fell asleep. The next thing she knew, it was morning.

I got a phone call that morning from a very excited little girl: "Auntie Marilyn, I DID IT! I really did it! I stayed at Grammy's house *all* night! And I didn't even ask to go home! I fell asleep and when I opened my eyes it was light outside!" She was incredibly proud of herself and filled with the intense joy only a five-year-old can possess. She had triumphed over a struggle that had vexed her for quite some time. She had every reason to be proud and joyful.

The same day that Jaclyn reached her milestone I finished a major project. It was something that I never thought I'd be able to do. It took months to complete, consumed a lot of energy, and required the help of many friends and colleagues. I was spent, but happy to have it behind me. Now it was time to move on to everything I had neglected while I was working on the project. So when Jaclyn called that morning with her announcement, I could relate to her feelings of triumphing over tough times. But I also felt a little jealous. After all, I had just accomplished a major feat just like she did. I figured I was entitled to that same sense of pride and joy.

I hung up the phone that morning and went to my desk where I had left the project when I finished it. I held it up proudly and admired the work I had done. I remembered the long road that it took to get there. I thought about the challenging moments, as well as how much I enjoyed doing it. I recalled the encouragement and help I received from friends and colleagues. I took it to the living room and put it in a place where I would see it frequently. Then I stepped back and said aloud to myself, to Jaclyn, and to the world, "I did it! I really did it!"

RING THE BELL THAT STILL CAN RING.

FORGET YOUR PERFECT OFFERING.

THERE IS A CRACK IN EVERYTHING.

THAT'S HOW THE LIGHT GETS IN.

Leonard Cohen

Marilyn Kielbasa is an editor, author, workshop facilitator, retreat leader, and piano teacher. She is an adjunct faculty member at Christ the King Seminary and St. Bernard School of Theology and Ministry and has been active in youth ministry and catechesis. She holds a Master of Arts in Music History and Literature from the University of Southern California.

Marilyn has written magazine articles, published courses, and several books, including *Ministry Resources for Pastoral Care*; *Prayer: Celebrating and Reflecting with Girls*; and *Community Building Ideas for Ministry with Young Teens*. She resides in Lackawanna, New York.

More Books in the GOD KNOWS Series...

GOD KNOWS Your Job Gets Old
12 *Ways to Enliven It*
ISBN: 1-893732-51-7 / 160 pages / $11.95

♦♦♦

GOD KNOWS Grandparents Make a Difference
Ways to Share Your Wisdom
ISBN: 1-893732-50-9 / 160 pages / $11.95

♦♦♦

GOD KNOWS Caregiving Can Pull You Apart
12 *Ways to Keep It All Together*
ISBN: 1-893732-44-4 / 160 pages / $11.95

♦♦♦

GOD KNOWS Parenting Is a Wild Ride

GOD KNOWS ... Always Easy

... .95

... .95

... .95

Simple Ways to Restore Your Balance
ISBN: 1-893732-35-5 / 160 pages / $11.95

♦♦♦

GOD KNOWS You're Grieving
Things to Do to Help You Through
ISBN: 1-893732-39-8 / 160 pages / $11.95

♦♦♦

GOD KNOWS You'd Like A New Body
12 *Ways to Befriend the One You've Got*
ISBN: 1-893732-37-1 / 160 pages / $11.95

♦♦♦

GOD KNOWS You Worry
10 *Ways to Put It Behind You*
ISBN: 1-893732-59-2 / 160 pages / $11.95

KEYCODE: F0S01040000